SHORT WAL

C000219958

Derby

Pubs

Charles Wildgoose

COUNTRYSIDE BOOKS
NEWBURY, BERKSHIRE

First Published 1995
© Charles Wildgoose 1995

COUNTRYSIDE BOOKS
3 Catherine Road
Newbury, Berkshire

ISBN 1 85306 332 0

For Katy and Jamie – with Love

Designed by Mon Mohan
Cover illustration by Colin Doggett
Photographs and maps by the author

Produced through MRM Associates Ltd., Reading
Typeset by Acorn Bookwork, Salisbury, Wiltshire
Printed by J.W. Arrowsmith Ltd., Bristol

Contents

Publisher's Note

We hope that you obtain considerable enjoyment from this book; great care has been taken in its preparation. However, changes of landlord and actual closures are sadly not uncommon. Likewise, although at the time of publication all routes followed public rights of way or permitted paths, diversion orders can be made and permissions withdrawn.

We cannot of course be held responsible for such diversion orders and any resultant inaccuracies in the text which result from these or any other changes to the routes nor any damage which might result from walkers trespassing on private property. We are anxious that all details covering the walks and the pubs are kept up to date and would therefore welcome information from readers which would be relevant to future editions.

① Little Hayfield

② Castleton

③ Tideswell

④ Grindleford

⑦ Cutthorpe

BUXTON

⑥ Baslow

CHESTERFIELD

⑤ Great Longstone

⑧ Rowsley

MATLOCK

⑨ Hartington

⑪ Wessington

⑩ Middleton-by-Wirksworth

⑫ Thorpe

⑮ Ambergate

⑬ Fenny Bentley

ASHBOURNE

⑰ Horsley

⑭ Clifton

⑯ Duffield

⑱ Ednaston

DERBY

⑲ Repton

⑳ Hartshorne

Area map showing locations of the walks.

Introduction

Derbyshire is a fascinating county and, hopefully, this book reflects that. Every time I go out with my rucksack I have a sense of anticipation – what will happen on today's walk, what will I see, what will the weather be like? Very, very rarely am I disappointed with a route as there is always something new to experience. I hope the 20 walks included here bring you that same sense of anticipation. If you enjoy them, then I have achieved something.

The distances vary from 1 ½ to 4 ¾ miles but none of them are hard or difficult walks. However, if you have no idea of your capabilities try the shorter ones first – you can always build up to the longer ones later. My aim was to devise 'easy' walks – this suggests walks on the level to me but anyone knowing Derbyshire will realise we have some hills, and some valleys, and some dales. In other words, on a few of the walks there is a little uphill work here and there. It can't be avoided if you want a circular walk so, again, if you've got doubts about what you can do, try the shorter walks first.

The pubs have been good fun to explore and I have coped quite well with all the food and real ale I have felt compelled to try on your behalf. The landlords (and landladies) are all prepared for you to contact them to ask to park at their pub while you walk. There should be no problem with this, but you will appreciate that these pubs are featured because they are good ones. This means that they very often get very busy, especially on Sundays. It would be advisable, therefore, to bear this in mind when planning your walk. Personally, I do prefer to park away from the pub if possible – it gives me a little more flexibility.

When entering the pubs, please take off your muddy boots and shoes. It only needs one unfortunate experience to spoil things for other walkers.

The opening times (and the mealtimes) quoted in the book were correct when I visited them. Things change though and there is no harm in confirming opening hours and the times at which food is served, especially if you are thinking of going for a walk during the week or on a summer evening.

All the routes have been checked, but it is advisable to equip yourself with the appropriate OS map. This will be a back-up in case a hedge disappears or a crop is planted across the path. Whilst on the topic of equipment, it is possible that you could get away with walking in trainers but I would not recommend it – I much prefer boots or walking shoes. The only time I use trainers is when I'm going for a stroll on paths I know will be dry and will have a good, flat, surface.

I should like to thank my little band of checkers who went out and walked all these routes to make sure they made sense. Without them my task would have been so much more difficult. So, a heartfelt thank-you to Jackie Gurnhill, Paul Hopkins, Paul and Linda Stanley, Frank Ogden, John Bradley, Bryan and Muriel Crapper, Greg and Elsie Boam, Bob, Margaret and Laura Bacon, Jamie Wildgoose, Matt McKenzie, Julia Davis and last, but definitely not least, Chris Gale (aka the M.L.). You'll all be pleased to know I won't be phoning you again making demands on your time – for a few months at least.

My final thank-you goes to Balkees. Once again she has been there to advise, cajole and sustain me whilst I have written this book. She has thankfully developed a taste for real ale as well as an interest in the Derbyshire dialect – at last, she now knows what 'gerr 'em in, duck' means. Enjoy your walking.

Charles Wildgoose
Spring 1995

Little Hayfield
The Lantern Pike

1

It would be easy to pass the Lantern Pike whilst driving from Chapel-en-le-Frith to Glossop. The A624, which links the towns, is a fast road and you can see the pub and be past it before you realise – this would be a pity. The pub has quite a history. In 1927 the landlady was found dead in the pub with her throat cut. About £35 was stolen. Within hours a neighbour had been charged with murder. Just five months later he was hanged. In the 1960s the Lantern Pike was the local for the original scriptwriter of *Coronation Street*. Apparently many of the cast in the initial programmes were based on characters who used to drink in the Lantern Pike at that time.

This is a friendly pub and well worth the visit. The food is fairly priced with something for everyone. Besides salads and sandwiches there are traditional meals such as home-made steak and kidney pie, lasagne verdi, plaice and scampi or, if you prefer something a little different, dishes like cod and prawn crumble, Mexican pork, chicken breast in cream and chicken zingari are available on the menu at different times. For the real ale fan there is a difficult choice between Boddingtons Bitter, Flowers IPA and Timothy Taylor Landlord. For the cider drinker, try the Gaymer's Olde English. En suite accommodation is also available here.

During the week the Lantern Pike is open from 11.30 am to 3 pm and then 6 pm to 11 pm, but at weekends the pub is open on Saturday from 11.30 am to 11 pm and on Sunday from noon to 10.30 pm. Food is served during the week from noon until 2.30 pm and then from 6 pm to 9.30 pm, and on Saturday and Sunday from noon until 9.30 pm.

Telephone: 01663 747590.

How to get there: Little Hayfield is on the A624, north of Hayfield. It is 5 miles from Chapel-en-le-Frith and 3 miles from Glossop.

Parking: There is parking for only five or six cars in front of the pub and another four or five down Clough Lane at the side. Don't park further down Clough Lane, though, because it is difficult to turn round. Many visitors park along the main road just before the pub. You can park in one of the pub's car parks while you walk as long as you ask first. Alternatively, park in Hayfield at the Sett Valley information centre. The walk passes this.

Length of the walk: 3 ¾ miles. Map: OS Outdoor Leisure 1 Dark Peak Area (inn GR 035882).

This is an interesting town and country walk, with plenty of variety. Although there is a climb, you will be rewarded with a marvellous view of both Hayfield and Little Hayfield and the hills around.

The Walk

Walk down Clough Lane beside the Lantern Pike. Just before the right-hand bend climb the stile on the left. Cross the footbridge a few yards away. Follow the path away from the stream. This levels out and leads to a stile in the wall. Climb this onto the lane. Turn right for 5 yards, then left along a grassy track. Pass through a gateway soon after. Stay on the track as it bears round to the left, ignoring the gate into the field at this point. To your right Lantern Pike rises 1,200 ft above sea level. Follow the path between walls and then between a fence and a wall. Enter a long field, which narrows as you proceed. Walk towards the far end. At the end the path runs alongside a wall on your right, with houses on the other side. Climb the stile and turn left on the lane. At the end of the lane turn left along the main road – not left up Swallow House Crescent. This road leads under the A624.

After passing 1 and 2 Tollbar Cottages at the end of Swallow House Lane, turn right down the road towards the church. Pass the Pack Horse on the opposite side of the road and keep on into Market Street. Beyond the cottages known as 1 to 5 The Bear Pits on your right, bear (no pun intended!) right over the river Sett to the church. There is an attractive view downstream to the back of The Bear Pits. Turn right between the Bulls Head and the church. Pass Steeple End Fold on your left and Hayfield Conservative Club on your right. Cross the A624, carefully, to the car park opposite and the Sett Valley information centre (toilets available).

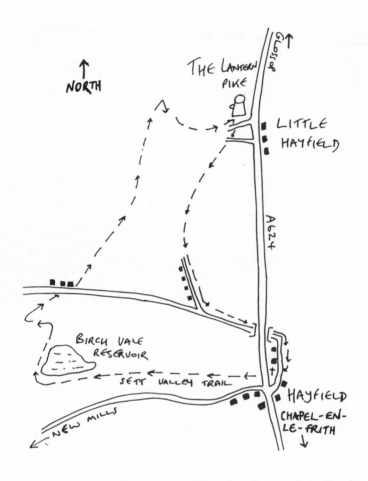

Turn right just beyond the centre, walking directly away from the church. This takes you through the car park and onto the Sett Valley Trail itself. Pass Bluebell Wood Nature Reserve on your right. Cross Slack's Crossing and ½ mile beyond turn right onto the path between Birch Vale reservoir and a factory. Follow this as it descends to the reservoir. Cross the bridge over the river, then walk straight forward up a bank to the far corner of the field. Follow the path between the wall and fence to a walled track. Turn left up this and follow it for 200 yards to a sharp bend to the right. Ignore the bridleway into the wood on your left. Climb the track you are on, to the road. The view of Hayfield and beyond improves. Turn right at the road for a few yards. Turn left, uphill, at the end of the terraced houses.

Climb up the rough track for 200 yards. Turn right along the level track to Higher Cliff Farm. Just before the house follow the waymarks to the right of

River Sett and the Bear Pits.

the property. The farmhouse should be above you on your left. At the end of the garden turn left through a gateway, then immediately right into the field. Walk away from the farmhouse along the right side of the field. A marvellous view of Hayfield appears before you. Cross the stile at the end of the field. From here descend diagonally left down the field in front. There is a distinct path which you should follow in this field, but 50 yards along it take a less distinct path, dropping slightly right through the gorse to the bottom. This takes you to a path running along the wall. If you find yourself in this field following a path which is not descending to the bottom you need to get down to the bottom of the field as soon as you can!

At the bottom of the field continue, with the wall on your right, into another field, on a grassy path, about 5 ft wide. This leads to a stile beside a gate. Cross this and proceed down to a gravel track. Turn left up this and walk behind the ruin of an old farmhouse to Firbob Cottage.

Just 5 yards beyond the small stone building on your right, turn sharp right to climb the stile into the field. Follow the path before bearing left then right. Descend along the paved path towards Clough Mill in the valley bottom – now converted into flats. Walk briefly alongside the river before crossing the footbridge to another bridge and onto the lane. Turn left and follow the lane as it winds uphill. About 100 yards beyond the mill pass through the small squeezer on the left, which brings you out in front of old cottages. Turn right up the lane to return to the Lantern Pike.

Castleton
The Peak Hotel

Castleton is one of the Peak District's honeypots. Tourists and walkers flock there in their thousands and it is not difficult to see why. As well as the many caverns and the remains of Peveril Castle, there is the countryside to explore or, just over the hill in Edale, the start of the Pennine Way. This runs for 250 miles or so northwards to Kirk Yetholm in Scotland.

The Peak Hotel is popular with locals and visitors alike. It is always a good sign when local people frequent a pub or hotel! The games room here used to be a pub known as the Butcher's Arms and the main part of the hotel was a pair of private houses. The car park opposite used to be another pub – there have been quite a few changes over the years. The hotel is busy and offers accommodation if you want to use Castleton as a base to explore the surrounding area.

Favourite food at the hotel includes the Sunday lunch as well as the battered haddock. There are occasional theme nights, featuring perhaps Mexican, Indian or Italian menus. Those who like a more straightforward meal are well catered for with chicken and mushroom pie, roast topside of beef, lemon sole poached in white wine or Peak Yorkshireman – a giant home-made Yorkshire Pudding filled with the chef's choice of filling. If you fancy something a bit spicier try the chilli con carne or the lasagne verdi.

The vegetarian will find dishes like broccoli and hazelnut bake or spinach and ricotta cannelloni. A children's menu offers Turkey Jetters, Peak Burger, Surf Burger (battered fishcake), cheese and tomato pizza and soup. There is a choice of beers from Tetley, Stones or Burton, and two ciders – Woodpecker and Gaymer's Olde English.

On Saturdays the hotel is open from 11.30 am to 11 pm, serving food from 12 noon until 2.30 pm and 6.30 pm until 9.30 pm. On a Sunday it is open from 12 noon until 3 pm and 7 pm until 10.30 pm, with food from 12 noon until 2.30 pm and 6.30 pm until 9.30 pm. During the week, opening times are 11.30 am to 3 pm and 5.30 pm to 11 pm, with food from 12 noon until 2.30 pm and 6.30 pm until 9.30 pm.

Telephone: 01433 620247.

How to get there: As you enter Castleton on the A625 from Hathersage and the east the Peak Hotel is on your left,with the car park on your right.

Parking: Parking is available in the car park opposite. Please ask first if you want to use it, while you walk. There is a car park and street parking in the village but you are best advised to get there fairly early – it does fill up very quickly.

Length of the walk: 3 ½ miles. Map: OS Outdoor Leisure 1 Dark Peak Area (inn GR 152830).

This is perhaps the most strenuous walk in the book, but well worth tackling. The route ascends through Winnats Pass with its unusual rock formations. You should be rewarded with some good views, a chance to see the Shivering Mountain at close quarters and one or two other unusual features.

The Walk

With the hotel behind you, turn left and walk along the main street of Castleton. The road turns first left then right. About 70 yards past the Castle pub on your left turn half-left. Follow the Riverside Walk towards Peak Cavern. This takes you between houses and then alongside the stream. Where the tarmac path joins a road bear right as though heading towards the cavern. Look out for Goose Hill ahead. Walk up this, ignoring the path to the cavern to the left. The tarmac lane rises past some cottages. Take the right fork when the lane splits. This soon becomes a rough track. Peveril Castle is above you to the left. Most of the ruins that are visible date from the late 12th century and are all that remain of the castle built by King Henry II.

Once you have passed through the farm gate walk ahead. Keeping the wall on your right, continue through the field. Ahead, to the right, is Winnats Pass. To the right of this is Mam Tor (or the Shivering Mountain). Our walk

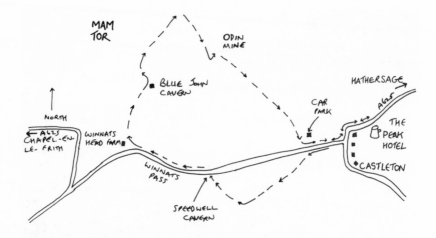

takes us up through the pass and then below Mam Tor. The path you are on bears right. Go through the stile at the side of a gate. From here walk on to reach the road. Turn left on the road to pass Speedwell Cavern. As you climb up the hill keep on the right side of the road. From the cavern the next ½ mile of walking is beside the road. There is a wide grass verge to begin with. Take your time as you walk up the slope. If you need a breather, turn round and look at the view behind. At weekends, in particular, there are likely to be hang gliders around – if the weather is good.

Just beyond a small cave, where a sandstone slab lies on the ground, look out for a stile on the right. Walk past this and stay beside the road. A second stile about 120 yards beyond the first is the one you want. Climb this and, with the wall on your left, proceed towards Winnats Head Farm. Shortly before the farm, bear right and walk alongside the farm fence. This is just about the highest point on the walk, so the rest is *nearly* all downhill! Mam Tor rises above you.

At the end of the farm buildings on your left turn right and walk directly away from the farm. This leads you to Blue John Cavern 300 yards away. As you walk towards the cavern (initially hidden from sight) you will see ahead one of the best known ridge walks in the Peak District. This runs from Mam Tor to Lose Hill, via Hollins Cross and Back Tor. Just over the ridge is Edale and the start of the Pennine Way – you can save this for another day.

Climb the stile to the left of Blue John Cavern. Walk in front of the building on your right, then follow the tarmac track round to the left to the road. Turn right on the road and begin the descent back to Castleton. Within a short distance the road reaches a dead-end. Walk to the bottom left-hand corner and pass through one of the gates or over the stile. You are now directly below Mam Tor. Stay on this road. As you will see, it is not what it was. It was last used by traffic in 1979, when it subsided. In some places

Winnats Pass, Castleton.

the road surface has dropped 5 or 6 ft. Follow the road round the right-hand bend. Peveril Castle is clearly visible above the village.

Pass the old road sign, with 'Sheffield', 'Hathersage', 'Chapel-en-le-Frith' and 'Sparrowpit' emblazoned on it. Go through the gate and read about the history of this area on the board. About 100 yards beyond the gate turn sharp left off the road. This path brings you to what remains of Odin Mine. Pass a large crushing stone on your right and cross a small brook by a footbridge. Stay on the well-defined path through some of the old spoil heaps. Continue in the direction of Castleton, crossing a step-over stile. Cross two more to reach Knowlegates Farm. Go in front of the farmhouse to a squeezer stile beside the farm gate. Press on, with Odin Sitch (the small brook) on your right. Pass through another squeezer and cross a field towards the large chimney, in the distance, in front of you. Go over another stile, before crossing Odin Sitch 30 yards away. Stay on the right side of this, then walk across a farm drive beside a cattle grid. With the watercourse on your left, walk through the longish field, then keep straight on in the next field. Finally, cross to the far corner of another field, before walking between walls out to the road.

From here turn left and walk back into the centre of the village and the Peak Hotel.

Tideswell
The George Hotel

Tideswell is something of a revelation. It is full of interest, not least being the 'Cathedral of the Peak' – the parish church of St John the Baptist. In addition, there are interesting little side streets and ginnels as well as the village shops. The George, next door to the church, was once an old coaching inn – the cobbled beer garden being the original courtyard. It was used for the Central TV serial *Yesterday's Dreams*, most of the filming taking place in the village or the pub. It is a friendly, cosy place, with a real log fire in the lounge in winter.

In addition to the Kimberley Best Bitter, Classic and Mild, Strongbow draught cider is available. Foodwise, there is plenty to choose from. For the traditionalists, steak and kidney pie, scampi, big beefy bangers and mixed grills are on offer. If you want something a little different, you could try the moussaka flan, leek and mushroom crumble or lamb and apricot pie. The children's menu comprises chicken, sausage or scampi. There are also special dishes for vegetarians. The hotel offers overnight accommodation.

The George is open for drinking from 11 am to 3 pm and 7 pm to 11 pm on Monday to Saturday, whilst on a Sunday it is open for the usual hours. Food is served from noon until 2 pm and from 7 pm to 9 pm every day.

Telephone: 01298 871382.

How to get there: From the A623 road, midway between Chapel-en-le-Frith and Baslow, follow the signs for Tideswell along the B6049. The George is on the right, ½ mile along this road.

Parking: There is a car park in front of the hotel which you can use while you walk, with the permission of the landlord. It is, however, just as easy to park in the street.

Length of the walk: 4 ¼ miles (or a shorter, 3 ½ miles, option). Map: OS Outdoor Leisure 24 White Peak Area (inn GR 153758).

The full walk is a mixture of tracks, paths, fields and a marvellous view of Miller's Dale. The shorter option saves a bit of uphill work but, as is often the case, misses out on the main view of the walk. Before you visit the hotel (or perhaps after) do visit the church.

The Walk

Turn right from the hotel on the main road as it winds through the village. Pass the church and National Westminster bank. Just beyond the war memorial bear right alongside the small green towards the Methodist church. About 10 yards later turn right into Hardy Lane. At the top turn left along the road until you pass Wellfield Terrace on the right. Turn right immediately beyond the terrace and walk up the field. At the top of the field climb the stile. Continue forward and cross a stile onto a track.

Turn left here. 150 yards later you reach a squeezer stile on your left. Opposite, on the right, is a gate. Climb the stile beside it. Walk on the right side of the next four fields.

In the fifth field bear half-left to the stile opposite. Keep on the same line through the next few fields. Follow the path and enter a long, narrow field stretching away to the left. Cross this and continue forward into the field in front, descending steadily as you go.

Walk towards the bottom left corner of the field past a mere. Climb the stile beyond this, then walk down the middle of the next field to cross a stile onto a track. Turn left along this for 600 yards. This track is an unclassified county road. It is part of the Limestone Way, the long distance path from Castleton to Rocester in Staffordshire, over 50 miles long.

After 600 yards the track meets another running from left to right. You now have a choice. The track to the left stays mainly on the level but misses out on the scenery further down the valley. The route to the right is ¾ mile longer but you will see some marvellous views. The longer route can be muddy, especially after wet weather.

The shorter route (to the left) is easy to follow. Walk along the track as it winds between the fields. After 500 yards (where the track turns right) ignore the stile on your left between two gates at a 90° angle to each other.

17

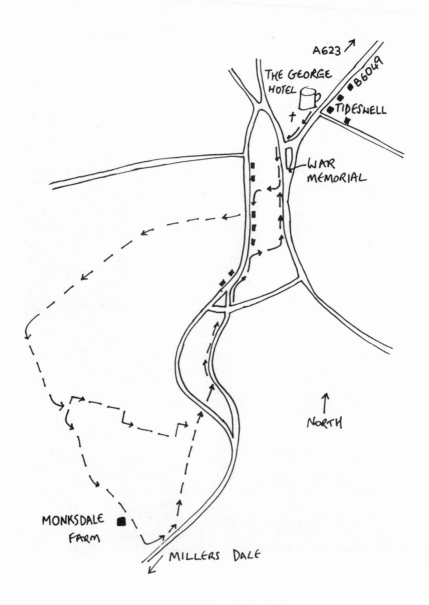

A623

THE GEORGE
HOTEL

B6049

● B6049

TIDESWELL

WAR
MEMORIAL

NORTH

MONKSDALE
FARM

MILLERS DALE

St John the Baptist church, Tideswell.

Continue along the track for another 600 yards, to a point where the track does another right turn. About 50 yards later a path crosses the track. Turn left over the stile and off the track. This stile is opposite two metal gates on the right side of the track. This is the point where the shorter route joins with the longer to lead back to Tideswell. Continue from the last paragraph.

The longer route (to the right) descends to a stile beside a gate across the track, 500 yards later. Cross this to descend still further. Ahead is the flat-topped hill known as Knot Low. The track bears left towards Monksdale farm. To your right is a bridge across the valley.

Walk along the track behind the farmhouse. Pass through a gate and walk for 15 yards into the farmyard. Then bear right, downhill, along the concrete driveway. After about 20 yards follow this round to the left, ignoring the path descending to the right. If you look up here you will see electricity cables overhead. Follow the line of these until they fork. Where they split keep straight ahead, passing a small breeze block building on your right: The driveway levels out. Walk along this for 200 yards. At the end of the drive cross the cattle grid to the lane. Note the attractive 'Monks Dale Farm' sign on the gate. Continue up the lane to the left for 100 yards. Pass through the stile on the left and walk towards the top right corner of the field. Pass through the squeezer stile 10 yards left of the gate.

Keep straight on – to the right of the hawthorns. Cross the stile ahead and then a ladder stile. Walk on the left side of the next two fields to a track. Cross to the stile opposite. Both long and short walks coincide to lead back to the George.

Cross the stile and walk along the left side of the field. This leads to a quiet lane. Cross this to walk along the left side of another field and onto a second lane. Walk left on this for ½ mile. Ahead are the outskirts of Tideswell. About 100 yards before you reach the first house on the edge of the village, ignore a road to the right and a track to the left. Turn right at the T-junction 100 yards later and walk in front of the houses. Stay on this road, ignoring all other roads off, until you reach Brookley Lane. Turn right down this, then left in front of the post office mailbox. Walk past the Horse and Jockey in the main street. Continue until you come back to the George.

Grindleford
The Sir William

There are few amongst us who have a hill as well as a hotel named after them. Sir William Chambers Bagshawe is one of the few. He was born in the 18th century and inherited an estate in Derbyshire when he was about 30 years old. Apparently he repaired the road up what is now Sir William Hill so that he could get from one part of his estate to the other. He had 23 children, 19 of whom survived him.

The hotel is at the bottom of the Sir William Hill in the village of Grindleford, in an area of excellent Peak District scenery. The Derwent flows through the village, there are lovely woodlands around and on the opposite side of the river from the hotel is Froggatt Edge. If you sit in the hotel garden when the weather is good you can gaze across towards the Edge whilst enjoying good food and drink.

Children are welcome in the hotel and their special menu comprises The Italian Job (cheese and tomato pizza), Seaside Special (fishcake), Chippy Chippy Bang Bang (sausage, egg and chips) and Treasure Chest (chicken nuggets). For adults, good traditional food is served, most of it home-cooked and with as many fresh vegetables as possible. Vegetarians are catered for with items like courgette and mushroom lasagne and broccoli and cheese bake. Lasagne, steak pie, Norfolk country pie, sandwiches,

21

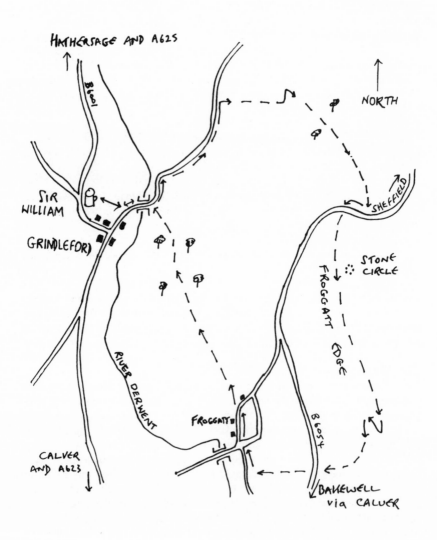

HATHERSAGE AND A625

B6001

SIR WILLIAM

GRINDLEFORD

NORTH

SHEFFIELD

STONE CIRCLE

FROGGATT EDGE

RIVER DERWENT

FROGGATT

CALVER AND A623

B6054

BAKEWELL via CALVER

omelettes, fisherman's crumble, plaice, gammon, roast chicken and sirloin steak all appear on the menu, as well as home-made sweets. Tetley and Burton Bitters are always for sale and in addition there are usually three guest beers, plus Gaymer's Olde English cider. The hotel has seven bedrooms.

The hotel is open for drinking from 11 am until 3 pm and 6 pm until 11 pm on Monday to Friday, from 11 am to 11 pm on Saturday, and from noon to 3 pm and 7 pm to 11 pm on Sunday. Food is available from noon until 2 pm every day and in the evening from 6.30 pm until 9.30 pm on Monday to Saturday or 7 pm until 9 pm on Sunday.

Telephone: 01433 630303.

How to get there: Grindleford lies between the A625 at Hathersage (2 ½ miles away) and the A623 Chapel-en-le-Frith to Baslow road. The Sir William is on the B6001 to the north of the village.

Parking: The hotel has a car park on either side. Please let the landlord know if you wish to park there while you walk. There is some parking available on the roads nearby.

Length of the walk: 4 ¾ miles. Map: OS Outdoor Leisure 24 White Peak Area (inn GR 243778).

This is one of the longest walks in the book, but the scenery is marvellous all the year round – definitely the Peak District at its best. The route zig-zags up to Froggatt Edge with its wide views. You return via the attractive village of Froggatt and the lovely Derwent valley.

The Walk

From the hotel entrance turn right. At the end of the car park, opposite the war memorial, turn right down the footpath to the road. Cross to the telephone box. Turn left to go over the river. Stay on the road and pass Toll Bar Cottage on your left, then the church on your right. Continue up the road past Nether Padley Farm on your left. Near this point make sure you are walking on the left side of the road. About 120 yards beyond Padley Road the main road disappears round a right-hand bend. Just before this, look out on the right side of the road for a footpath leading into a field. This is just before the Maynard Arms Country Hotel. Enter the field by the gate near the signpost dated 'July 5th 1912'. The path leads to the 'Froggatt Edge Road via Tedgness for Owler Bar, Totley and Sheffield'. You won't be going quite that far!

The path through the field rises to a gate. In the second field stay on the left to walk between a wall and a fence. This brings you to an unmade road. Turn left for 10 yards. Opposite Cayley Lodge, turn right to ascend between

Froggatt bridge

another wall and fence. Walk left along a second unmade road for 100 yards. Turn sharp right just past Rostherne along the path signposted 'Haywood Car Park, and Froggatt Edge'.

Initially this is a gravel path but it soon has a grass surface. Enter Haywood and ascend steadily. The path levels out and then descends slightly. Just after this, disregard the path that forks uphill to the left – stay on the grassier right fork. About 60 yards later ignore another path joining from the right. Continue to a disused quarry on the left. Shortly after, pass through a small gate beneath the electricity lines. Down to your right through the cutting in the trees is the Sir William across the valley.

Walk forward, ignoring paths to the car park. Around 50 yards beyond the gate the path levels out. Shortly after, descend down cobbled stones to a gateway. Pass through and cross the stream. Ascend the path beyond to the road. Turn right for about 50 yards. Pass through the kissing-gate on the left side of the road, onto the distinct footpath along Froggatt Edge. Follow this for the next mile or so and enjoy the marvellous views.

Some distance beyond another kissing-gate look out for a narrow grassy path to the left. This leads to a standing stone about 3 ft high, about 30 yards off the main path – part of an ancient stone circle. The other stones are nearby. Return to the main path.

After walking between some rocks 10 ft or so high, you go alongside a gritstone wall on the left. At the end of this take the path that cuts back (downhill) at an acute angle to the right. This takes you off the Edge below the path you were on. About 60 yards along this are some old millstones that have been cut but never used. This is a popular area for climbers and at weekends you are almost sure to see some on the rocks to your right. About 150 yards from the point where you left the main path along the Edge (and 50 yards before a high column of rock in front of you) turn left at a sharp angle off the path you are on. Descend the rocky path into the wood below, watching out for loose gravel as you go. Another path crosses from left to right as yours levels out. Climb the stile directly in front and descend through the wood.

You come out onto the B6054 rather abruptly. The Chequers Inn is to the right. Cross to the gate opposite and climb the stile beside it. Walk towards the ruin 20 yards away. Swing left down the middle of the field through the hawthorns.

Cross the stile beside the gate at the bottom of the field. Turn right along the lane past Meadow Croft. Continue to Froggatt Bridge on your left. Do not cross this – keep on the road to pass to the right of it. Then pass Bridge Foot Farm on your left. Walk along Hollowgate on the raised pavement. At the Wesleyan Reform chapel, on the right, cross the road. Keep left of Rose Cottage to walk along Spooner Lane. This becomes a track after a while. About 500 yards from the village pass through a squeezer by a gate and continue to the end of a wall on your right. Go diagonally right to a stile by a gateway 80 yards away. Walk on the left side of the field, after passing through the gateway. Follow the path along the paving stones to enter Froggatt Wood.

Follow the main path through the wood for ⅓ mile.

At the end of the wood keep on the left side of two fields to a stile on your left. Go through this and walk through the field to the far side. Turn left at the road, cross the Derwent and return to the Sir William by your outward route.

Great Longstone
The Crispin Inn

5

St Crispin was the patron saint of shoemakers and the link with a 20th century pub name appears to be that a bit of the pub is alleged to have been part of a 16th or 17th century monastery. The Crispin has been a pub or alehouse for 200 years at least. It is situated on the main street of Great Longstone, a village full of attractive buildings.

The landlord was formerly a butcher so you will not be surprised to hear he regards the Crispin steaks as the pub speciality. There is much more to choose from, at reasonable prices, including chicken chasseur, sandwiches, salads and vegetarian dishes such as spicy bean pot, vegetable rogan josh and spinach and ricotta cheese cannelloni. In addition, there are some interesting sweets – cappuccino ice-cream, American butterscotch pie and New York lemon cheesecake, to name but three. The children's menu includes chicken nuggets, fish fingers, sausage and scampi. The real ale on offer is Robinson's Best Bitter and Strongbow cider is also available.

The pub is open during the usual Sunday hours. For the rest of the week the times are 11.30 am to 3 pm and 6 pm to 11 pm. Meals are served from noon until 2 pm every day and from 7 pm until 9 pm on Monday to Thursday (9.30 pm on Friday, Saturday and Sunday).

Telephone: 01629 640237.

How to get there: From Ashford-in-the-Water (2 miles west of Bakewell via the A6) take the B6465 road to Monsal Head. Turn right here for Great Longstone. After passing through Little Longstone you reach the Crispin about a mile or so later, on your right, just after entering the village of Great Longstone.

Parking: There is a limited amount of parking in front of the pub. Parking on the roadside in the village is probably just as easy.

Length of the walk: 4 miles. Map: OS Outdoor Leisure 24 White Peak Area (inn GR 198718).

A walk with hardly any uphill work. Attractive scenery and the delightful village of Great Longstone. Local legend mentions something about 12 headless horsemen with a carriage and coffin in the vicinity of the stretch of path down towards the Monsal Trail – best not tackle this walk at dusk!

The Walk

Face the Crispin and walk along Station Road to the left of the pub. This is signposted 'Thornbridge Hall'. Pass the Methodist chapel. Immediately beyond Orchard House, turn left on the tarmac footpath between the hedges. About 100 yards later, turn right to walk along the path, with the playing field on your left. At the road cross over and walk down a path, with a beech hedge on your left. Cross another road and walk to the squeezer stile ahead, to the fields beyond. Bear half-right from the stile to cross the step-over stile halfway down the wall on your right. Continue to the far corner of the next field. At this point go out onto the road and turn left, immediately, through the gate. Then walk down the right side of the field to the bridge over the Monsal Trail. Cross this and immediately turn left onto the Trail.

Once on the Trail turn right and walk along it for 1 mile. Away to your left is Longstone Edge. The Trail crosses two roads, one 500 yards after the other. Just under 300 yards beyond the second one look out on your left, across the other side of a field, for Toll Bar House. Leave the Trail at the signpost for 'Rowland', to walk across the field towards the house. Turn left at the road in front of the house. About 80 yards later cross the road to the gate and climb over the stile. From here walk straight forward along the track towards the clump of trees ahead. As you ascend steadily through the field aim to walk alongside the wall in front of the trees. When you reach it keep it on your right through the next few fields. Look out for a step-over stile on your right at the end of the wall. Continue along the distinct path to the road.

Turn left on the road for a short distance, then right along the lane to Rowland. Walk through the village. Where the road turns right take the

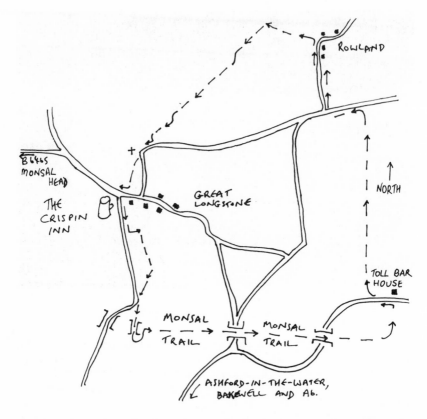

squeezer stile on the left (beside a gate), then go over another stile on the right almost immediately. From the second stile turn left under the trees. At the end of the field go through the stile and walk across the field in front to a step-over stile. Walk forward about 60 yards into the field, then turn left to go along a wide, grassy track. Keep to the left of a water trough as you go. This leads you onto a track between parallel field walls 50 or so yards apart. At the end of this narrow field pass through a squeezer by a gate. Walk on the track in front of you. This bears left until you reach a walled track. At a point where the walls are quite high (and with a steepish bank over the wall on your left) look out on the right for a stile. Go through this and follow the distinct path forward. Make sure you cross the step-over stile and do not go through the gate further up the wall. Walk diagonally across the next field, to the gateway with gritstone gateposts – the walls are limestone – in the corner opposite, then forward to the bottom corner of the next field. Get onto the walled track and turn left. Stay on the track as it turns first right and then left to arrive at the road.

Toll Bar House, near Great Longstone.

Turn right to the church and go into the churchyard by the stile on the right. Then, keeping the church on your right, walk to the kissing-gate at the far side of the churchyard. This leads to a tarmac path which in turn leads to another kissing-gate. Turn left down the short lane to the road. Finally, turn right along the road to the Crispin.

Baslow
The Robin Hood Inn

6

The Robin Hood Inn stands in an area actually known as Robin Hood. There is even a Robin Hood Farm nearby, shown on OS maps. But which came first, the inn or the place name, or was there some connection with the man himself? After all, Little John is buried only 6 miles away at Hathersage. There has apparently been a hostelry on the same spot as the present Robin Hood Inn since the 17th century. It was thatched at one time but little more is known of its history. It is certainly well known, and popular with climbers who frequent Birchen Edge and walkers exploring the area around the inn. At weekends and bank holidays it can be very busy hereabouts.

Strongbow cider is on sale here, as well as Riding Traditional Bitter, Riding Dark Mild, Old Baily and Mansfield cask bitter. The menu gives a good choice, for example, scampi, gammon, chicken Kiev, lasagne, beefburgers, quiche, steak and kidney pie, vegetable lasagne, shepherd's pie, sirloin steak, chilli con carne, meat and potato pie, broccoli and Stilton pie, leek and Stilton bake, chip butties, toasties and sandwiches. Children's portions of most meals are available.

The inn is open all day on a Saturday (from 11.30 am until 11 pm) and on Sunday from 12 noon until 3 pm and then from 7 pm until 10.30 pm. During the week it is open from 11.30 am to 3.30 pm and 6.30 pm to

11 pm. Meals are served on a Saturday from 11.30 am until 2 pm and then from 6 pm until 9 pm, then for the remaining six days of the week from noon until 2 pm and 6.30 pm until 9 pm (except Sunday evening).
Telephone: 01246 583186.

How to get there: The Robin Hood is about 1 ½ miles east of Baslow. Turn off the A619 Baslow to Chesterfield road onto the B6050, signposted 'Cutthorpe' and 'Whittington'. The inn is on your left almost immediately.

Parking: The Robin Hood has a small car park and the landlord would prefer you to park in the public car park adjoining the inn. On Saturdays and Sundays he opens the field opposite the pub as a car park so, as an alternative, you can park there.

Length of the walk: 4 ¼ miles. Map: OS Outdoor Leisure 24 White Peak Area (inn GR 280721).

This is a walk with splendid views and relatively easy moorland walking. You can throw in Robin Hood, Lord Nelson and the Duke of Wellington (three great names from England's past) for good measure. Please note that occasionally, at times of high fire risk, it will not be possible to walk this route.

The Walk

Walk out of the Birchen Edge car park, next to the pub. Turn left up the road, away from the Robin Hood. Just beyond the house on the left turn left off the road. Negotiate the step-over stile to enter the Eastern Moors Estate. Walk on the well-defined path in front, alongside the wall, rising steadily as you go. The path bears gradually round to the left. When you reach a squarish rock, about 2 ft high, on the left of the path, keep straight on, ignoring the less distinct path climbing upwards on the right. The path then forks again. Stay on the level, ignoring another path climbing to the right. At a hawthorn tree the path forks a third time. Go to the right.

The sandy and rocky path ascends towards Birchen Edge. This gritstone rockface is popular with climbers, as you may see. In the distance on your left is Chatsworth Park. The path you are on runs quite near to the Edge. Above you will see the monument erected in memory of Admiral Lord Nelson. The path continues below the monument until you reach the end of the Edge. There are one or two paths in this area, but if you stay within 20 yards of the rocks you should not lose your way.

The path you are on should now be heading in the direction of the Sheffield road on the hillside in front of you. Not far beyond the Edge you should pass a large boulder on the left, with the initials 'MF' above those of 'DS'. This boulder is 6 ft high and approximately 15 ft wide – not easy to

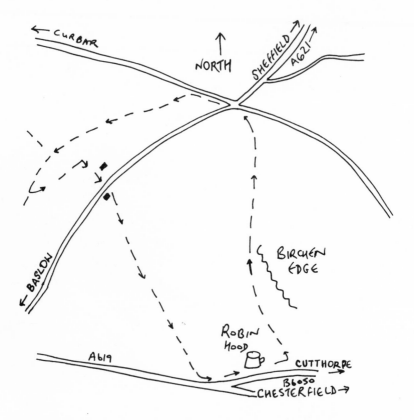

miss. Continue past this, still on your left, towards the road. After a time, the path broadens out and can be quite boggy in places. Generally, it continues in a straight line towards the Sheffield road. About ½ mile after the boulder the path reaches a ladder stile. Climb this, turn left and cross the main road.

Take the Curbar road for 200 yards or so, rising as you go. Then, on your left, pass through a gate onto a track across the moorland. Walk along this ancient trackway until you reach an old stone marked 'Chesterfield Roade'. Keep on the track past it. On your left across the valley, Birchen Edge can be seen, with Gardoms Edge below. Ahead of you is a monument erected in memory of the Duke of Wellington.

As you near this monument, away to your right is the Eagle Stone, a squarish stone about 15 ft high. The view from Wellington's Monument is worth enjoying. Shortly after, the track you are on is joined by another coming in from the right, from the direction of the Eagle Stone. Stay on the track you are on and descend towards Baslow in the valley in front. After passing a disused quarry on the right, the track leads towards a gate. Before you reach it turn sharp left, to go alongside a wall and fence on your right. You will then be walking just below the track you have been on, to your left.

This path will eventually lead you down into the valley bottom. Initially though, it is level for 200 yards or so. It then passes between oak trees and rocks before bearing right downhill. There is a wall within about 20 yards on your right as you descend. This eventually leads you towards a house ahead on your left. Climb over the step-over stile to the right of the house. Follow the path between the hedge and the wall,then continue round to the left, alongside metal railings, to an old bridge. Above this is another bridge to the house! The waters of the Bar Brook pass beneath both bridges.

Once over the bridge, turn right to the A621, the busy Sheffield/Baslow road. Take care when crossing. The stile you need is just to the left of Cupola Cottage on the opposite side of the road. Once over the stile the path bears right, behind the cottage. Walk alongside the garden on your right. At the end of the fence keep forward, rising slowly through the silver birches. Where the corner of a stone wall juts out on your right, keep straight on, to pass through a gap in the wall. Stay on the path as it goes through an area of relatively open ground. It then bears left slightly, to proceed through more silver birch trees.

Pass through an open gateway in a stone wall. Another lovely view opens out on your right-hand side. Go through another gap. Away to your left is a largish outcrop of rocks. Head straight forward through the field in front of you. The buildings in the vicinity of the Robin Hood should become visible ahead as you proceed. You need to walk just to the right of them towards the road. Eventually, you may be able to discern a path on the ground. A stile brings you onto the road. Turn left. About 200 yards later you will reach the inn.

Cutthorpe
The Gate Inn

The Gate Inn was built halfway through the last century but little is known of its history. On a clear day, though, you can see for miles – in fact, the landlord reckons that the power stations on the Trent, 35 miles away to the south, are visible some days. Certainly, there are wide views to the north-east when the weather is clear.

The inn offers good value for money and is certainly popular – it is a friendly, busy pub. The dining room is a no-smoking area, by the way. Children are welcome and they are catered for with chicken nuggets and jumbo fish fingers, or they can have small portions of some of the items on the menu. There are many favourites on offer, such as mixed grill, steak and kidney pie, gammon steak, burger, giant Cumberland hot dog, breaded plaice fillet and grilled sirloin steak. Then there are Q L salads (Quite Large), such as Cheddar or cottage cheese, home-boiled ham, home-roasted topside of beef or prawn. Sandwiches are also available, with or without chips, as well as jacket potatoes. In addition, there is a blackboard offering specials, such as beef in ale with dumplings or cold chicken marinated in honey and spiced in Tandoori. So, a wide range of different types of food to suit all tastes, with even more choice on the evening menu.

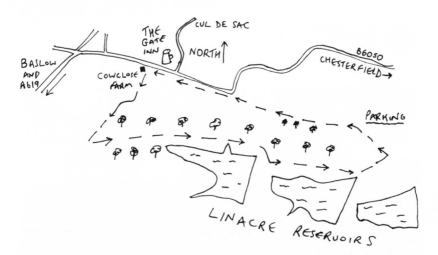

Real ale is sold, namely Boddingtons, Stones, Flowers Original and Mansfield Riding, and Strongbow cider.

The Gate is open from 11.30 am to 3 pm and 6 pm to 11 pm on Monday to Saturday, with the usual hours on a Sunday. Food is served daily from noon until 2 pm and on Wednesday, Thursday, Friday and Saturday evenings from 7 pm to 9 pm.

Telephone: 01246 276923.

How to get there: The Gate stands beside the B6050 1 mile west of Cutthorpe, which is north-west of Chesterfield. Approaching from the A619 Baslow-Chesterfield road, turn off at Robin Hood onto the B6050, signposted 'Cutthorpe' and 'Whittington'. Follow the Cutthorpe signs to reach The Gate about 4 miles later.

Parking: There is a car park behind the pub and it is possible to park at the front and the side. If you want to leave your car while you walk, please ask the landlord first. The pub does get busy, though, so try and arrive in good time to get a parking place. Alternatively, you can travel about ½ mile down the road towards Chesterfield and turn right to park in one of the Linacre Reservoirs car parks.

Length of the walk: 2½ miles. Map: OS Outdoor Leisure 24 White Peak Area (inn GR 375734).

This is a short walk which acts as an introduction to the Linacre Reservoirs. As you will see as you follow the route, there are more paths to explore and further visits to the area are certainly worth considering. Today's walk, though, is fairly leisurely, through the woods and by the water.

Chesterfield from Linacre Reservoirs.

The Walk

Facing away from the Gate Inn, turn right towards Cowclose Farm. This is 50 yards or so away along the road. Turn left and pass through the squeezer stile beside the gate. Walk along the driveway to another squeezer stile – also beside a gate. Continue forward towards the track, with a hedge on both sides. You may have to pass through a gate to get onto the track. Stay on the track as it bends round to the right to a gate. Climb the step-over stile to the left of it. Walk up the right-hand side of the field in front of you. At the end of the field cross the ladder stile on your right. From here bear half-left to pass through some hawthorns, then continue towards the far end of the trees running along the bottom of the field. This means you will be walking diagonally down the field. Just before the end of the trees look for a stile. Cross this. The next stile you need is just under 100 yards away, down the wall on your left. This takes you into the wood on your left.

Once you have crossed the stile into the wood, follow the path through the trees for the next ½ mile. Ignore a substantial wooden bridge after 200 yards or so. As you pass through the wood the path becomes much better surfaced.

At the end of the reservoir on your right walk down the shallow steps. This reservoir was the second one to be built and holds (at most) 126 million gallons of water. Keep on along the main path through the wood. The route does not cross the embankment to the right to the other side of the reservoir. The main path takes you on through the trees, with the middle reservoir below to your right. At the end of the middle reservoir the path you are on has dropped in height so you are now walking nearer to the water level. You walk past the overflow on your right and go through a gateway. A footpath turns right to cross the embankment but, as before, ignore this. You should take the path leading slightly left, uphill.

The path continues to ascend as you walk. Stay on it, passing two or three other paths dropping downhill to your right. Also pass the steps rising to the left slightly later. The path then levels out and leads you to a kissing-gate beside a wooden farm gate. Pass through this onto the tarmac drive beyond. Some 200 yards downhill to your right are some toilets – not always open. Our route climbs to the left however, so follow the tarmac lane to the left. About 200 yards later pass a car park on the left. Continue to ascend for another 200 yards until you pass a picnic and amenity area on your right.

Pass this area and, 100 yards beyond, take the bridleway ahead, where the lane bears right. Walk alongside a wood on your left. At the end of the wood pass through a gate into a field. Go straight forward. This leads you to a track. Continue for the next 500 yards or so until you reach Pratthall. Pass a grass triangle on your right. At the road turn left. Walk back to the Gate Inn, 200 yards ahead.

⑧ Rowsley
The Grouse and Claret

The Grouse and Claret has an excellent reputation for its food, its accommodation and it even has facilities for touring caravans. In addition, it is almost literally a stone's throw from the Peak District; private fishing is available for anyone staying there and Haddon Hall and Chatsworth are about five minutes away by car. It is the sort of place where you could spend a week, let alone half a day, walking. The pub started off life as the Rowsley Railway Tea Room before becoming the Station Hotel. It subsequently changed its name again, this time to the Grouse and Claret. The railway station has been closed for some years now but the pub has survived and goes from strength to strength. It is certainly an imposing building as you drive along the A6 through Rowsley. The name 'Grouse and Claret' is, by the way, the name of a fishing fly and has nothing to do with a day's shooting followed by a tipple afterwards.

A large range of meals is available, including Tom Tiddlers Menu for the under 12s. There is also a children's playground. For the over 12s there is a snacks and cold menu comprising items like a glass of prawns or a ploughman's lunch. The main course menu offers 10 oz rump steak, 8 oz sirloin steak, a large mixed grill, 8 oz gammon steak, seafood platter, Whitby scampi and half a roast chicken. Then there is a vegetarian selection, also

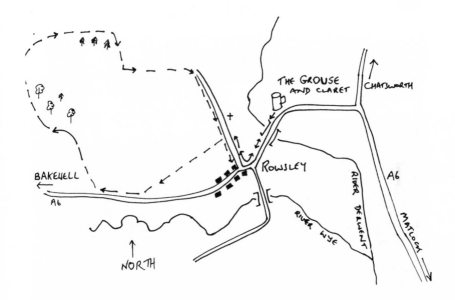

hot plate specials and blackboard dishes such as the Grouse and Claret sausage and Old Bailey beef. So there is plenty to choose from. The Mansfield award-winning beers served include Mansfield Cask Bitter and Riding Bitter, as well as Old Baily. Then there are seasonal beers such as Red Admiral and Red Stag. Strongbow and Woodpecker ciders are also sold.

The pub is open at weekends for most of the day. On Saturday drinks are sold from 11 am to 11 pm and food from 12 noon to 9.30 pm, whereas on Sundays drinks are available from 12 noon to 10.30 pm, food until 9.30 pm. During the week the hours are reduced somewhat.

Telephone: 01629 733233.

How to get there: The Grouse and Claret is very easy to find, being at the side of the A6 in Rowsley. The village is partway between Matlock and Bakewell.

Parking: There is plenty of space to park at the pub, as well as on-street in the village.

Length of the walk: 2 ¾ miles. Map: OS Outdoor Leisure 24 White Peak Area (inn GR 257660).

An old well, Rowsley.

This is a lovely walk all the year round, but especially in May when the bluebells are out – they are quite magnificent. This will be a good walk if you have young children. There is plenty of birdlife to be seen (especially pheasants) and the scenery is lovely.

The Walk

Walk out onto the A6 from the Grouse and Claret and turn right. Cross over the river Derwent and after passing the Peacock Hotel, turn right up Church Lane. Ignore the stile on your right after 150 yards. Look out for a squeezer stile (and signpost) 50 yards later, on the left, in front of a house, after a gradual right bend. Pass through this and walk away from the road to another stile at the far side of the garden. Head for a third stile directly in front of you. This brings you into the fields. Keeping the wall on your left, walk to the stile ahead. The A6 runs parallel to you. Beyond this lies the wooded mound of Peak Tor – an unusual name as a tor is usually a rocky outcrop or cliff face. Once through the stile at the end of the first field, walk towards and pass through the next two fields, then bear half-left to the step-over stile to take you onto the A6.

Turn right along the road. At the end of the field turn right up the wide track. As you walk along this the noise of the traffic fades away. For the next ¾ mile no further instructions are required. All you have to do is stay on the track. It climbs the hillside steadily, with fields on the left and woodland on your right. There is plenty of wildlife about – partridges, rabbits, magpies, wood pigeons and pheasants can all be seen from time to time.

After the track descends slightly you reach another one coming in from the left. Turn right here and 20 or so yards later a view opens up on your left towards Bakewell. At this point, as you look down the valley, Haddon Hall is ¾ mile to your left and Chatsworth House 2 ½ miles to your right.

As you continue on your way, bear right to take the bridleway leading uphill. Another track to your left goes down to Bakewell and the other, just to the right of the Bakewell route, into the wood, eventually leads to Chatsworth. Ascend the bridleway on your right and look out in the far distance for the towers of Riber Castle 6 miles away. Rowsley can also be seen in the valley, as well as Peak Tor. Where the track forks keep straight ahead into the trees. The next 400 yards is through woodland and can be muddy at times. The last wooded stretch on your right is fairly shady and spooky. Even on the sunniest of days it can be very dark under the conifers. In bluebell time each year this stretch of woodland is quite spectacular.

At the end of the wood, with a field directly in front of you, swing downhill to the right. Follow this rough track until it reaches the buildings of Rowsley, then continue to descend down Church Lane as far as the A6. Turn left here and return to the Grouse and Claret.

Hartington
⑨

The Devonshire Arms

Hartington lies just over ½ mile to the east of the river Dove as it meanders from the hills above Buxton to join the Trent a couple of miles north of Burton upon Trent. The village is blessed with a small cheese shop just the other side of the duckpond from the Devonshire Arms – lovers of Stilton will be pleased to know this and can also be reassured that Stilton is usually somewhere on the menu at the pub.

At the Devonshire Arms children are welcome. There is a family room (formerly stables) and children's meals – chips with fish fingers, sausage or egg – are available. For the adults (or perhaps children with hearty appetites) there is a good choice of food. Home-made soup (excellent to warm you on winter days) served with a doorstep of bread sounds appetising. Then there are the main meals – chicken pieces with chips and salad, chicken Kiev, breaded plaice or scampi, ham, egg and chips, sirloin steak, gammon steak, lasagne, Stroganoff, curry, chilli and ploughman's lunches (with a choice of roast beef, ham, Cheddar or, of course, Hartington Stilton). Then there are jacket potatoes with different fillings and sandwiches, as well as various specials which change regularly. Bass, Burton and Tetley real ales are on offer, as well as Dry Blackthorn cider. Overnight accommodation is available.

The opening times change from summer to winter. Broadly though, from May to mid-September the Devonshire Arms is open seven days a week from noon until 10.30 pm on Sunday and 11 pm for the rest of the week. Food is served from noon until 9 pm on Sundays, 9.30 pm on the other days. During the winter the weekday opening times are reduced (Monday to Friday) so that the pub is usually closed from 3 pm to 7 pm.

Telephone: 01298 84232.

How to get there: Hartington lies a couple of miles to the west of the A515, midway between Ashbourne and Buxton. Follow the B5054 into the village and the pub is on the left-hand side in the centre.

Parking: There is only space for a few cars in front of the pub. It is easier to park in the village streets or in the car park at the south-western side of Hartington. It does get very busy in the village, so do get there early if you want to park and have a meal after your walk. Sundays and bank holidays are very, very popular!

Length of the walk: 3 miles. Map: OS Outdoor Leisure 24 White Peak Area (inn GR 128604).

The village of Hartington is one of the most popular starting points for walks into Beresford Dale, Wolfscote Dale and Dovedale. This route, however, is a relatively short one which takes you down to see the delights of Beresford Dale before leading you up and away to the quieter fields to the south-east of the village.

The Walk

With your back to the Devonshire Arms, turn left along the road. Pass the bank on your left and the Charles Cotton Hotel on your right. Near the outskirts of the village turn left beside the toilets at the Peak District and N.C. Society signpost. After passing through the small gate behind the toilets, continue on the path to the right. This path is easy to follow for the first few fields as it heads away from the village. Ahead are the attractive hills of Narrowdale. Cross the walled track. In the first field beyond the track the path is visible on the ground and leads to a squeezer stile in a tumbled-down wall. From here, head slightly right towards two gates. Pass through the stile beside the gate on the left. Continue forward along the path, round the bottom of a small hill known as Pennilow. Keep on in the general direction of a tower on the wooded outcrop ahead. Pass through a stile onto a distinct path leading into the trees. You are now entering Beresford Dale.

Initially you walk on the left side of the river, but then you cross to the other side by a footbridge at Pike Pool. This dale is where the ancestors of Thomas Beresford (see walk 13) lived. Ideally you should try and walk this

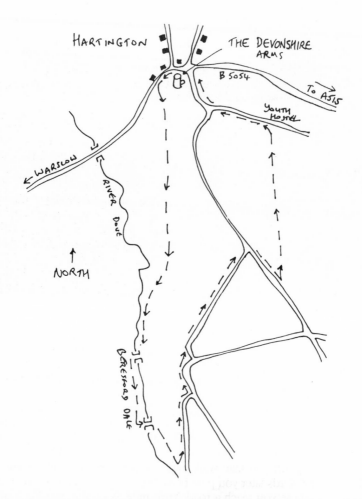

path when no-one else is about. It is a lovely lush, green dale – quite different from the other dales further downstream.

Cross the river Dove again, by a second footbridge, this time from the right side to the left. Notice the unusual squeezer stile on the far side, complete with the cut-out section at the bottom for your boot. From here, turn right across the meadow. On the far side of the field pass through the squeezer and walk towards the bridge. Do not cross it, though. Turn left on the track that leads uphill. Before you do this, take the opportunity to look downstream. This is Wolfscote Dale – very different from Beresford Dale.

Keep on the stony, walled track leading uphill. Ignore a track from the right after 100 yards and keep straight on. About 200 yards later turn right

Hartington youth hostel

with the track and walk to a quiet country lane. Turn left along this. In wet weather the roadside is full of yellow snails. As you proceed along the lane the countryside beyond Hartington is visible. Look carefully for a squeezer stile on your left as the lane bears round to the right.

You have two options here. Either squeeze through the stile and walk to another stile by the gate 40 yards away or keep on the lane and turn left to come to the same point. It may help you make up your mind to know the second squeezer stile is narrow.

Whichever option you take walk away from the second stile along the track. Some 400 yards later you pass between two farm buildings. Then 250 yards beyond these you reach a road. Turn right along this, passing a small clump of trees over the wall on your left after 200 yards. Continue to the end of the field in which the trees stand. At the end of the field is a step-over stile (signposted at present). Climb over this and, with your back to the wall, walk half-left. This leads you through a gap in the wall about 40 yards from the road and the clump of trees on your left. Head straight forward, keeping a telegraph post in the middle of the field on your left. As you get to the upper corner of this second field you will see it comes to a point. This leads you via an open gateway onto a walled green lane. Stay on this for 600 yards until you reach the road with the impressive Youth Hostel in front of you. From this point turn left down the road into the village. At the bottom turn left into the centre of Hartington and return to the Devonshire Arms.

10 Middleton-by-Wirksworth
The Rising Sun

Middleton-by-Wirksworth is one of three Middletons in Derbyshire. The other two, Stoney Middleton and Middleton-by-Youlgreave, are in the Peak District. Middleton-by-Wirksworth is, however, just a mile outside. D. H. Lawrence lived here during the First World War. Tradition has it that Lawrence and his wife were verbally abused when she had to register regularly at Wirksworth police station because she was German.

The Rising Sun stands on the crossroads at the southern end of the village. It is popular with both locals and visitors and also offers overnight accommodation. The High Peak Trail is only a few hundred yards away and on sunny days and weekends there are lots of people in the pub. It was originally a farmhouse, the farm buildings located where the car park now is. The buildings were demolished and the farmhouse converted within living memory. It is said the ghost of a young girl haunts the pub. Indeed, in the 1950s the landlord at that time discovered a secret bedroom that had been boarded up . . no-one knows why.

There is a good selection of food. 'Children's Tempters' such as sausage, beefburger, chicken nuggets, fish fingers or scampi, all served with fries and peas, are available and children under 8 years or 8 stone are rewarded for an empty plate! The choice for adults is varied and tasty and ranges from the straightforward (a steakwich served in a bun with fries and side salad) to the more unusual – chicken breast filled with prawn and lobster). What else? Well, you will find seafood, poultry and vegetarian meals, followed by 'Sweet and Sticky'. Then there is a daily special, such as corned beef and onion pie. Every Sunday a traditional lunch is available. The mixed grills are popular and Friday is fresh fish day. Tetley, Pedigree and Burton ales are on offer, together with Gaymer's Olde English cider.

The hours that the pub is open can fluctuate, depending on the weather. As a guideline, assume you can drink from 11.30 am to 3 pm and from 6 pm to 11 pm during the week, then on Saturday from 12 noon to 3 pm and 6 pm to 11 pm. Sundays have the usual licensing hours. Food is available every lunchtime from noon until 2 pm, then in the evenings from 6 pm to 8.30 pm, except Sunday when meals are served from 7 pm. Evening meals are popular so it may be necessary to book.

Telephone: 01629 822420.

How to get there: The Rising Sun is 1 mile north-west of Wirksworth on the B5023. It stands at the crossroads where this road crosses the B5035.

Parking: The car park is in front of the pub. You can also park at Middleton Top visitor centre 500 yards away. To get to Middleton Top take the B5035 beside the pub, towards Ashbourne. After passing under a bridge turn right for the visitor centre.

Length of the walk: 3 miles. Map: OS Outdoor Leisure 24 White Peak Area (inn GR 279553).

This is a walk with excellent views, using the High Peak Trail for part of the way. It is a route that gives an insight into the industrial past of the area. Quarrymen, leadminers and railwaymen earned their living around here. Some quarries still operate and, of course, the land continues to provide a living for local farmers.

The Walk

With your back to the Rising Sun, walk left along the road to the end of the car park. Cross the road and turn right to the crossroads 50 yards later. Follow the B5023 for Wirksworth and Duffield. About 150 yards beyond the crossroads pass under the bridge and turn left, immediately, to get onto the High Peak Trail. Turn right down the Trail under the trees. The Trail levels out and on your right is a large winding wheel.

Pass a disused quarry on your left. Down to your right, off the Trail, is the National Stone Centre with Wirksworth beyond. As you continue you can see Black Rocks ahead. Stay on the Trail passing houses on your right. Cross the main road from Cromford, then go over another (minor) road beyond this. About 50 yards further on turn left through a gap off the Trail. Walk

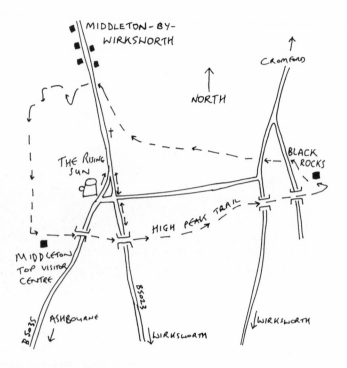

downhill towards Steeple Arch cemetery. Black Rocks information centre is a little further along the Trail.

Turn left immediately beyond the cemetery. Walk towards the road ahead. Cross this and enter the yard beyond. Walk forward, with the buildings to your right, and leave the yard. Stay on the path in front (ignoring a path veering right). The path rises to a squeezer onto a rough track. Pass through to the stile beside a gatepost opposite. Continue forward, then bear slightly left between the hummocks. These contain spoil from old lead workings. In spring and summer the flowers here are surprisingly varied. Many of them thrive on the lead in the area. Pass a capped mineshaft – some of these are hundreds of feet deep. Take care to avoid them, particularly if they are uncapped or look unsafe.

A few hundred yards beyond the shaft pass through the squeezer beside the stone ruin. The path runs along the wallside and fence on the left. After passing through another stile, continue towards the church some 500 yards ahead. Go through another stile onto a more distinct path. It becomes walled. Stay on this as it changes to a track, passing the church and the old rectory.

At the T-junction with the road, turn left for 20 yards to the main village street. Cross this and climb Sandy Hill past some attractive cottages. Some 50 yards after the road the path levels out. Turn sharply right in front of the

Middleton Top.

house with the number '6' on it. Pass the house numbered '7'. Keep straight on as the tarmac lane becomes a rough track by a garage. At the side of a gate negotiate the stile on your left. Follow the path up the hillside as it turns first right, then left.

The path comes to a track. Turn left and then right about 50 yards later. On your right is an old quarry. At the end of it climb the stile on your left. Follow the track that stretches out ahead through the fields to Middleton Top.

At the bottom of the hill turn right where a track comes in from the left, then cross the stile beside the gate and descend onto the Trail. There are toilets and a shop here. You can also hire a bike if you like. Beyond the car park is a view indicator, showing points of interest, the most distant being Sutton Coldfield TV mast, 35 miles away.

Walk along the Trail, with the chimney on your right. This takes you to the top of Middleton Incline. In the engine house is a beam winding engine that used to pull wagons up the slope. The Engine House opens every Sunday (with engine static) from 10.30 am to 5 pm. It also opens on the first Saturday of every month (with engine in motion).

Pass through the gate by the signal and descend steadily. Ahead is Bolehill TV transmitter and Black Rocks. Pass over the Middleton to Ashbourne road. Marvellous views open out, of Matlock and Riber Castle. Descend through a cutting and then under a bridge. Cross another road before leaving the Trail by the path that brought you onto it. Turn right under the bridge and return to the Rising Sun.

⑪ Wessington
The Horse and Jockey

The Horse and Jockey was a coaching inn from 1645. Before this it was an alehouse for the local farmers and workers. The oak beams testify to its age and add to its atmosphere and no ancient pub would be worth its salt without a ghost – a friendly ghost here, though – Esmeralda, the lady in white.

Children are welcome in the Horse and Jockey and, as well as a playground, have their own menu, with grub such as fish fingers and beefburgers on offer. Adults have a good choice, too, and the menu includes sirloin steak, salmon and broccoli parcels and steak au poivre. Vegetarians are catered for with Orchard Steak (wheat and vegetables in a burger-style bun) and Covent Garden Bun (puff pastry filled with vegetables in a rich tomato sauce). Tetley Bitter, Ind Coope Burton Ale and a draught mild are on offer plus Gaymer's Olde English cider. Overnight accommodation is also available.

The pub is open during the week from 11.30 am to 3 pm and 6.30 pm to 11 pm (food from 11.30 am to 2.30 pm and 6.30 pm to 10 pm), on Saturday from 11.30 am to 4 pm and 6.30 pm to 11 pm (food from 11.30 am to 3 pm and 6.30 pm to 10 pm) and on Sunday from 12 noon to

3 pm and 7 pm to 10.30pm (food is available from noon until 2.30pm and 6.30 pm until 9.30 pm).

Telephone: 01773 833197.

How to get there: Wessington is midway between Matlock and Alfreton on the A615. The Horse and Jockey is in the centre of the village and can't be missed.

Parking: The landlord is happy for you to park at the pub while you walk, but ask first, if possible. There is also street parking available in Wessington.

Length of the walk: 3 ¾ miles. Map: OS Pathfinder 794 Crich and Bull-bridge (inn GR 370578).

This is a walk through lovely countryside south-west of Ogston Reservoir. You are unlikely to meet many walkers but it is an area growing in popularity. There is a chapel ruin to visit, too – and very little uphill work!

The Walk

With your back to the pub, turn right and leave the car park. Keep right, into Brackenfield Lane. Stay on this road until it takes you into the countryside. Pass Roadnook Farm and 450 yards later pass a signpost and stile on the right. Keep on the lane. At Brackenfield Green keep left, walking gently uphill. Pass Greenbank Farm on your left after 100 yards. Another 100 yards later pass Brackenfield Methodist church built in 1890.

The road forks 80 yards beyond the church. Take the left fork to the T-junction. Turn left again, but only for 15 yards, then turn right along the track that is signed 'Carr Lane'. A few yards along the lane you get a glimpse of Ogston Reservoir to your right. Where the track wheels left to pass behind the bungalows, keep straight forward towards the farm buildings in front. Stay on the track past the farm buildings. A couple of hundred yards later the track brings you into an open field on the left. Turn left at this point to walk up the hedgeside. At the top of the field pass through the stile onto the path between the hedge and wall.

Near the end of the path, to your left, is the hamlet of Mathersgrave. Samuel Mather was buried here in the 17th century. At the roadside is a stone marked 'SM 1643'. There are conflicting tales about Samuel Mather – some say he was hanged for stealing, others that he was a suicide. Whatever happened, he was buried at the crossroads. Some stories mention that whilst being taken for burial a raven or crow landed on his body, a bad omen indeed!

At the lane turn right. A marvellous view opens out on your right. On the ridge is the line of Ryknield Way, a Roman road. Some 80 yards after joining the lane turn left immediately beyond a small water trough, through a

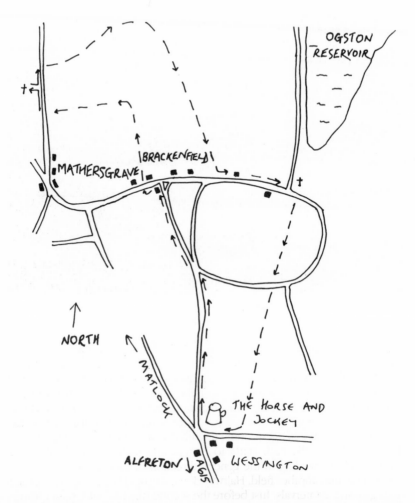

OGSTON
RESERVOIR

BRACKENFIELD

MATHERSGRAVE

NORTH

MATLOCK

THE HORSE AND
JOCKEY

ALFRETON A615 WESSINGTON

gateway. Walk up the left side of the field towards the conifers, then walk up the left side of the trees to another trough. Just 20 or so yards beyond this pass through a small gate on the right. This leads to the ruin of Trinity Chapel. The chapel has suffered from vandalism, which is a great shame. There is no roof but evidence shows that this chapel is over 400 years old. It probably stands on the site of an older church dating back even earlier. Some of the paths you are using are, therefore, likely to have been used for over 1,000 years.

Return to the road. With the trough to your right, turn left away from Mathersgrave for 200 yards. As you go, you pass the end of the field on your right. Opposite this on your left is a stone step stile and a signpost – ignore

Ogston reservoir.

these. Walk on until you come to the end of a second field. Turn right through the gap, at a signpost. Walk down the field, with the hedge on your left. You will be heading towards the right-hand side of the water visible ahead. At the bottom corner of the field walk half-left over the wooden footbridge. Continue directly away from this for 15 yards. This brings you into a small clearing between hedges. From here, continue forward on the left-hand side of the hedge running downhill away from you. About 30 yards down this hedge the path starts to bear round to the right slightly. You should now be heading in the general direction of Ogston Reservoir.

Continue into another field. Halfway down the field is a line of four or five trees growing at intervals. Just before the second tree (an oak), pass through the stone stile. Walk across the field on your right, at an acute angle from the path you have been on. Enter and pass through the wood. Turn left once you come out into the field. Walk round the edge to a stile at the corner of the wood. Continue forward through the next few fields. The wood is 100 yards or so away across the field on your left. The path will lead you alongside the trees again. Where they end, cross a stile. Keep on the left side of the next field until you reach a track. Follow this to a lane. Turn left, passing Teapot Farm. Take care on the corner just beyond here.

At Brackenfield church walk down Butterfield Lane. Opposite the main door of the church, pass through the stile on your right. Follow the direction of the 'Wessington' signpost towards the far corner of the field. Cross a low stone slab bridge as you go. This is easy to spot because of the 3 ft high posts at each of the four corners. Cross the bridge and bear slightly right towards a stile ahead in the broken hedge. After crossing this, the temptation is to cross the stile 10 yards or so away, directly in front – don't! Bear slightly left of the stile and walk forward, with the hedge on your right. Continue forward towards a gate at the end of the field. There is a stile beside it and you should climb this into another lane.

Cross to the stile opposite. There is a small hazel tree growing here. Look out for hazelnuts during the summer and early autumn. Bear half-right to the gateway opposite, then continue to the stile at the other side of the field. After crossing Winny Brook, walk up the field, with the hedge on your right. Catch your breath at the top of the field by turning round to look at the lovely view. Cross the track to the stile opposite. From here, walk diagonally across the field towards the clump of trees. At the road (Back Lane) turn and walk uphill to return to the Horse and Jockey.

⓬ Thorpe
The Dog and Partridge

The hotel has a copy of a brochure issued by the Dog and Partridge in the 1920s. At that time the telephone number was Ashbourne 95 and a double bedroom cost 6/6d a night. A fire in the bedroom, for one night, was 2/6d extra, but baths were free. The brochure goes on to say that 'the accommodation is fitted throughout with electric light.' Going back to the 18th century a Lord Torrington dined on 'bad oatcakes at the poor alehouse in Spend Lane – the Dog and Partridge by name'.

These days, however, the cuisine is excellent. There is a good choice at reasonable prices, including children's favourites. The older generation will find basket meals, salads, chilli con carne, quiche, vegetable lasagne, plaice, haddock and scampi on offer. There is also home-made steak and kidney pie, which, apparently, draws people from afar. Then there are 'specials', such as chicken and broccoli bake, lamb casserole with Stilton dumplings, and cod and prawn crumble. Home Bitter, Pedigree and Theakston XB are for sale, plus Dry Blackthorn cider.

The opening times vary from summer to winter but you can usually assume that you can get a drink from 11.30 am to 3 pm on Monday to Saturday, and on Sunday from noon to 3 pm and 7 pm to 10.30 pm.

However, on some days in summer, especially Saturdays and bank holidays, the Dog and Partridge may be open nearly all day from 11 am.

Telephone: 01335 350235.

How to get there: The Dog and Partridge is 3 miles north-west of Ashbourne and is signposted from the A515. The hotel lies ½ mile to the east of the village, on the road between Thorpe and the A515 near Tissington.

Parking: The hotel has a large car park. Alternatively, leave your car in the Narlows Lane public car park nearby.

Length of the walk: 3 ½ miles (or a shorter walk of 2 miles). Map: OS Outdoor Leisure 24 White Peak Area (inn GR 163504).

The longer walk passes through spectacular countryside – the view of Ilam and the Dove valley is breathtaking. The shorter option misses a marvellous view of the dale – but also avoids a climb out of the valley!

The Walk

From the entrance to the hotel walk down the lane signposted 'Tissington 1 ½, Newhaven 7 and Buxton 18'. About 120 yards later leave the lane and keep to the right at the grass triangle. Follow the sign to the 'Tissington Trail'. Walk past Station House on the right and go through the car park onto the Trail. Turn right along the Trail and within 200 yards look out for signposts on either side. Take the footpath to the right through the kissing-gate and walk forward through the field. Aim for a stile at the top of this field, 10 yards to the right of the electricity posts in the hedge. Cross the next field, heading slightly right, to reach the road. A mile away is the unmistakable sight of Thorpe Cloud rising like a pyramid.

Cross the road carefully and walk along the lane ahead. Pass The Firs, on your left. Stay on the lane for 600 yards, firstly on the level and then descending to the edge of Thorpe. About 30 yards beyond Stoney Cottage, at the bottom of the lane, turn left onto the grassy area. Walk between the willows and cross a plank bridge in a clearing. Continue forward, ignoring the open ground uphill to the right. Stay on the 4 ft wide path in this area. It is boggy on either side. This leads forward into the trees and begins to ascend. Pass a stone cottage above to your right. Continue along the gravel path, with the church to your right. Where the path levels keep along the track with a grass middle section. Pass a house on your left and then a red-brick house shortly after. The track bears right to the road. Turn right along this to St Leonard's church. This is well worth visiting.

Follow the road round to the left, to walk away from the church (ignoring a road to the right). Pass the old school house, dated 1887. At the bend in the lane, 100 yards later, there are two options.

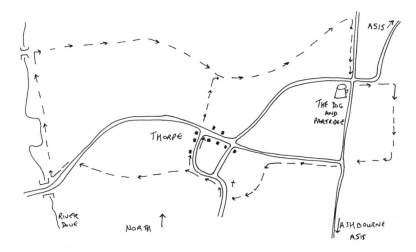

You can turn right for the 2 mile walk or keep straight on along the footpath for the 3 ½ mile route.

For the shorter walk, turn right along the road and pass Digby House. Cross the road at the T-junction to the Wintercroft Lane car park. Passing the toilets on your left, walk forward and go through the stile into Thorpe Pastures. Walk on the gravel track for 100 yards. Thorpe Cloud is now much nearer. At the end of the wall on your right turn right for the rest of the walk and continue from the final paragraph.

For the longer walk, take the footpath straight ahead through the small stile. Pass through a gate, then climb a stile and walk forward through two fields. Aim just to the right of the farm across a third field. Go through the stile leading across a drive, then squeeze through a stile beside the farm gate ahead. Walk towards the valley ahead. Thorpe Cloud is to your right, with Bunster Hill to the left of it. As you descend, pass through a stile in the middle of the wall ahead. Ahead is a splendid view of the valley, with the village of Ilam the focal point.

The path descends steeply towards the cattle grid to the right of the buildings below and joins the road 15 yards right of the grid. Turn left for 100 yards. Immediately before the bridge, take the grassy track to the right of the road. Within a few yards climb the stile on your right. Keep left alongside the ditch and enter a second field, alongside the river. Cross a third field, bearing slightly right. Walk gradually away from the river before re-joining it 100 yards later. Pass between the river and the small plantation of trees. In the fourth field walk towards the footbridge.

There are toilets if you cross the footbridge and then turn left and, sometimes, refreshments.

With the footbridge on your left, turn right and walk directly away from

the river. Thorpe Cloud (pictured above) rises on the left. There have been problems with erosion on this hillside and the National Trust is encouraging the grass to regenerate itself. So, walk along the stony path for 150 or so yards from the bridge, then bear slightly left uphill along the distinct path. Do not continue along the less obvious path straight ahead, which is slightly lower on the hillside than the one you want. The higher of the two paths proceeds towards a small outcrop on the left. Continue ascending until the path begins to level out. Keeping a stone outbuilding on your right, follow the path round to the left to a kissing-gate. Pass through this to ascend steadily away from the wall towards a disused quarry, 250 yards ahead. Go just to the right of the quarry. Ignore the gravel track heading right towards Thorpe. Walk forward towards the wall jutting out into the field and keep to the left of this. There is a dead tree stump in the wall. Thorpe Cloud is now behind you and Thorpe is a field away on your right.

Both routes join at this point. Walking beside the wall on your right, pass behind the Peveril of the Peak Hotel. Ignore the stile on your right 50 yards beyond it. Shortly after look to your left for a rifle range. You may have noticed red flags flying earlier – a warning that live bullets are used. However, the line of the path is perfectly safe. At the end of the wall negotiate the stiles in the small enclosure to enter the field beyond. Walk alongside the hedge on your right. At the end of the hedge, 170 yards later, pass through a stile into another field. Walk along the left side of this field, and the next, to reach a quiet country lane. Turn right to return to the Dog and Partridge, 400 yards later.

Fenny Bentley
13 The Coach and Horses

Motorists on the A515 often pass through the village of Fenny Bentley before they know it. They may have caught a glimpse of the Coach and Horses, Bentley Old Hall and the church of St Edmund, but then they're gone. What a lot they miss.

The Coach and Horses is a late 16th century building and, as its name perhaps suggests, it has long been in the business of quenching the thirst of travellers. It was originally a coaching inn and will, no doubt, have seen many a weary traveller call in for a pint of ale. Much larger inside than it looks from the outside, it has a friendly atmosphere and plenty of choice when it comes to food. There are over 60 items to choose from – starters, salads, fish dishes and steaks. Children are catered for with their own menu, which includes fish fingers, beefburgers, eggs, pizza and chicken nuggets. There are also three different 'specials' each day, including a roast. The real ale fans have something of a treat in store – not only does the Coach and Horses offer Bass bitter (plus three lagers, Worthington Keg and draught Guinness) they also have some locally brewed beers for sale. One is Hartington Bitter, brewed in the village of the same name 5 or 6 miles north. The others are Black Bull Bitter and Owd Shrovetider Strong Ale, brewed just a few hundred yards away across the fields by the Black Bull Brewery.

This brewery promises you 'Real Ale – No Bull'. The Owd Shrovetider, in particular, is an excellent strong ale, to be drunk after the walk, definitely not before.

Food is available on Monday to Saturday from 11.30 am to 2.30 pm and in the evening from 6.30 pm to 9.30 pm. Meals on Sundays are from noon to 2.30 pm and from 7 pm to 9.30 pm. The pub is open for drinking from 11.30 am to 2.30 pm and 6.30 pm to 11 pm on Monday to Saturday, with the usual opening hours on a Sunday.

Telephone: 01335 350246.

How to get there: Fenny Bentley lies 2 miles north of Ashbourne on the A515 Buxton to Ashbourne road.

Parking: You can leave your car in the pub car park while you walk if you ask first. There is also a little roadside parking 300 yards away. Turn left immediately beyond the church, into Ashes Lane. You can park on this road in the vicinity of the church.

Length of the walk: 2 ¼ miles. Maps: OS Outdoor Leisure 24 White Peak Area and Pathfinder 810 Ashbourne and the Churnet Valley (inn GR 175500).

A short walk at the southern tip of the Peak District. The old part of the village is full of history. The Tissington Trail provides an easy ½ mile of walking.

The Walk

With the Coach and Horses behind you, turn right up the road for 200 yards. On your right is Cherry Orchard Farm. This includes part of the remains of Bentley Old Hall and is a rather striking building. The Hall was originally the home of Thomas and Agnes Beresford and they are remembered in the church across the road. Thomas fought at Agincourt in 1415. Cross the road just before the telephone box, taking care as you do so. Keep on the road and then pass through the stile on your left at the side of the church lychgate. Walk through the churchyard, keeping the church on your right. Inside is the shrouded tomb of Thomas and Agnes Beresford, supposedly one of only two such tombs in the country. You can see their 21 children around the base. Thomas and Agnes were the author's great-great-great-great-great-great-great-great-great-great-great-great-great-great grandparents. The church is also the focal point of the Beresford Society. Members from all over the world come to Fenny Bentley to visit the tomb of their ancestors.

Leave the churchyard by the metal gates at the end of the tarmac path. Turn left along the road, passing the houses on your right. Just beyond them take the footpath on the right, signposted 'Thorpe'. After passing through

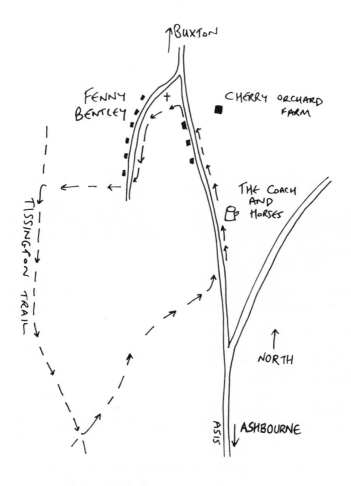

the kissing-gate, continue up the right-hand side of the field. Go through a narrow metal gate and continue ahead on the path. Where the hedge bears right, away from you, keep straight ahead. Once through the gap in the hedge walk forward, with a hedge now on your left. Ahead in the distance is Thorpe Cloud, the impressive looking hill, about a mile away. After passing through a stile at the end of the field, walk forward to the valley bottom. Cross the footbridge over Wash Brook. The kissing-gate at the top of the field you are now in is not easy to see from here, but, by walking just to the left of straight ahead, you should find it. The gate is approximately 60 yards to the right of the top left-hand corner of the field. Keep to the right of the hawthorns in the field as you ascend.

Pass through the kissing-gate onto the Tissington Trail. Turn left and stay

Cherry Orchard Farm.

on the Trail for just over ½ mile. At this point a path crosses the Trail. Turn left here for Fenny Bentley. Walk down the banking from the Trail and into the field. Bear slightly left downhill towards the hedgerow that runs from the brook up the other side of the valley. Cross the bridge over the brook. Walk up the left side of the hedge. Once through the old stone squeezer stile, bear left towards Ashes Farm. Keep just to the right of the farm. Walk to the metal farm gate, after passing the garden on your left. Cross the stile to the right of the gate. Bear half-right to the metal farm gate 100 yards or so away and cross the stile at the left-hand side. From here you must walk just to the left of the bungalow facing you. Aim towards the right-hand corner of the hedge and fence jutting out into the field to the left of the bungalow. Once you have crossed the field, go down the side of the hedge and fence and then pass through the gap/gateway at the end of the hedge. Walk very slightly right to the stile in the fence between the two properties in front. Cross the stile before going over a solid old stone slab bridge, then turn left along the road. The Coach and Horses is only 100 yards or so away.

⓮ Clifton
The Cock Inn

Clifton is rather off the beaten track for walkers. The walk and the pub are fascinating, though, and well worth visiting.

The Cock is an old coaching inn whose age is unknown. The low beams in the bar certainly indicate that this is an ancient place and the pub has lots of character. It doesn't rely on gimmicks – this is a place where you can eat a good, reasonably priced, meal and have an enjoyable drink. Much of the fruit and salad is home grown so there is a seasonal flavour to the food. One of the most unusual sweets you are likely to taste in any pub is rhubarb and strawberry pie – you can get it here, though. The children's menu includes jumbo fish fingers, sausage, egg and chicken nuggets, all served with chips and peas. For adults, in addition to sandwiches and sweets, there is a wide choice of appetising meals, including chicken, plaice, gammon and pineapple and vegetarian lasagne. Dry Blackthorn cider is for sale, together with M&B Mild and Bass for the real ale drinkers.

The inn is closed on Monday (except bank holidays). During the rest of the week, except Sunday when it is open for the normal hours, the Cock is open from 11 am to 2.30 pm and 7 pm to 11 pm. Food is available each lunchtime (except Monday) from noon until 2 pm and on Thursday to Sunday evenings from 7 pm to 9 pm.

Telephone: 01335 342654.

How to get there: Clifton is on the A515 just south of Ashbourne. Follow the sign for 'Clifton Village'. The Cock Inn is opposite the church.

Parking: There is a large car park behind the inn so there is no problem with parking. Street parking is also available.

Length of the walk: 4 ¾ miles. Map: OS Pathfinder 810 Ashbourne and the Churnet Valley (inn GR 166448).

This route is full of interest in an easily walked area – there is only one, short, climb. You cross into Staffordshire, to Church Mayfield, with its interesting church, and walk by the Dove to the delightful village of Snelston, back in Derbyshire. On the return route, there is a chance to see a rare clapper stile.

As Shrovetide Football is played in Ashbourne on Shrove Tuesday and Ash Wednesday, it is perhaps inadvisable to tackle this walk on those days.

The Walk

From the inn face the church and turn right along the road, 50 yards later turn right down the road to Mayfield. On your right after 80 yards is the 'goal' for the Ashbourne Shrovetide football match, a 6 ft high rock. It marks the site of Old Clifton Mill and is one of two goals in the Shrovetide game. The other is at Sturston Mill 2½ miles away – the game is played between these goals.

About 30 yards beyond the goal turn left off the road along the tarmac lane. Continue, with a 6 ft high wall on your left and fields on your right. Follow the lane round to the right. Cross the river Dove into Staffordshire. Pass to the left of a red-brick house. Continue towards the factory buildings. Head forward along South View, then follow the road as it winds between the ends of two terraces of houses. Turn left beyond them and then right after 10 yards, over a footbridge. Bear left then quickly right. The footpath leads to a terrace of red-brick houses.

At the lane turn left. Pass the vicarage. This is Church Mayfield with an interesting contrast between old and new properties. Walk past the church porch to the tower. The holes in the tower door were caused by musket balls fired by Roundheads from the hillside above, during the Civil War. According to tradition, they were aiming at Royalists hiding in the churchyard. Return to the porch and walk back to the road.

Turn right and pass Manor Farm. Beyond this (where the lane turns right) pass through the stile on your left. Enter the field and walk down the left side. Stay on the left in a second and third field. In the fourth walk alongside an embankment. As the river bears left, keep forward towards a gateway 80 yards from the river. Ignore a second gateway 70 yards to the right of the first. In the fifth field walk towards the far end. This becomes narrower –

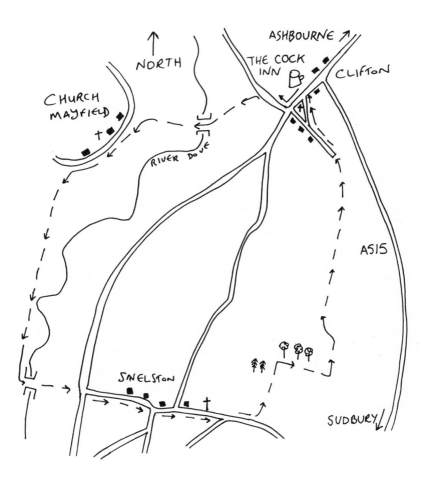

pass through the squeezer beside a gate. Walk straight across the sixth field. In the next field (the seventh!) bear slightly left. Keep right of a hawthorn in this field, though. This leads to an eighth field, with the path above the river. There is a weir to your left. Pass through a stile on your left in the hedge and walk between river and hedge for 30 yards, then climb another stile and bear left alongside the river round a bend.

When you see a bridge 200 yards away slightly to the right ahead, walk across to it. This is Toadhole footbridge – a lovely place to rest. Cross back into Derbyshire. From the bridge, bear slightly left to the gate on the other side of the field. This leads to a track and then to a road. Opposite is Littlefield Lane (this may not be signed). Walk along this for 500 yards into

The gatehouse of Snelston Hall.

Snelston. At the war memorial turn left. Pass the green corrugated village hall – something of a contrast to the other red-brick buildings in this lovely village. Continue along the road – ignoring the 'Clifton' road to the left. After passing the church, you will see the gatehouse of Snelston Hall. At the grass triangle 200 yards beyond this, keep straight on under the trees.

Some 200 yards beyond the triangle pass through the squeezer on your left beside a gate. Walk into the field and bear half-right. This leads to a gap between the trees on the far side of the field. Initially, this will not be visible because of the rising ground ahead. As you progress you should see it. Climb the stile beside the gate. Walk up the field ahead. Keep just right of the monkey puzzle trees. These are impressive – just look at the size of the tree trunks. When you are level with the plantation walk forward to a grassy track about 20 yards from the wood. The walk turns right along this.

Before you go along the track, walk forward towards the wood – and the stile. Initially you may not realise there is a stile, as it looks just like a fence. However, this is a rare clapper stile, apparently one of only three in the country.

To return to the route, walk up the grassy track, alongside the wood. After 300 yards you reach a farm gate between attractive gateposts. The path does not pass through the gate, however, but goes 15 yards to the right. Walk forward, keeping the metal fence on your left. About 200 yards away is a step-over stile in the hedge. Cross this, turn immediately left and walk through the gate. Continue forward from the gate, heading just slightly left of straight ahead. Keep to the left of the pair of oak trees (which are very close together) 50 yards from the gate – one is behind the other, so you cannot see them both. Descend through the middle of the field ahead. At the lowest point climb over the stile, then head forward, keeping the field boundary on your right for 200 yards. In the far corner cross the footbridge. Walk alongside the small stream to your left. Follow this to the corner of the field where it narrows. Cross the fence onto the old road. The busy A515 is just to your right.

Walk along the old road. Pass by the cemetery on the left. Further on pass the Wesleyan chapel and Hollies Close. At the war memorial bear right and return to the Cock Inn.

Ⓟ Ambergate
The Hurt Arms Hotel

Ambergate appears to have got its name fairly recently (well, last century) from the tollgates that used to stand in the vicinity of the Hurt Arms. These were on the turnpike road near the river Amber – hence Ambergate(s). A late 19th century photograph exists, showing the tollgates near to the recently built hotel. The Hurt Arms is, therefore, just over 100 years old. It stands prominently at the side of the A6 and provides a good starting point for a number of walks in the vicinity. The front of the menu proclaims that the hotel is the 'Gateway to the Peak District' and it is difficult to disagree, the scenery being just as good as anything you get another 10 miles north in the Peak District itself.

There is a wide choice of food at the Hurt Arms, but don't expect your meal to be ready in five minutes – all the ingredients are freshly cooked and this takes time. The restaurant is a non-smoking area, by the way. There are 15 starters, and when you study the main items you will have plenty to mull over. You will have to decide between scampi, battered cod, grilled trout with almonds (plus three more fish dishes), or sirloin and rump steaks, Monster Grill (steak, gammon, lamb chop, sausage, liver, egg and onion rings), Barnsley chop, or, for vegetarians, vegetable lasagne, deep-fried breaded mushrooms, mushroom and cheese omelette or mushroom Stroganoff. Then there are Derbyshire platters, one, for example, with two cheeses, another with honey roast ham. Roast dinners are served every lunchtime, too. These are best sellers, with pork, beef and turkey to choose from. The home-made steak pies are popular as well. Steak-lovers should bear in mind that Tuesdays and Fridays are 'Crazy Steak Nights' at the Hurt Arms when the steaks are cheaper than other nights. Children have their own menu and a play area outside.

Lunch is served from 12 noon until 2 pm every day with evening meals available from 6.15 pm until 9.30 pm (except on Sunday when food is served from 7 pm until 9 pm). The Hurt Arms opens for drinks from 11.30 am to 3 pm and from 6 pm to 11 pm, Monday to Friday. On Saturday they open nearly all day from 11.30 am until 11 pm. The usual times apply on Sunday.

Strong real ale is the order of the day at the Hurt Arms – Theakston Best and XB. Overnight accommodation is available.

Telephone: 01773 852006.

How to get there: The Hurt Arms Hotel is on the A6 about halfway between Matlock and Derby.

Parking: There is a large car park at the hotel. The landlord has no objection to you leaving your vehicle there while you walk.

Length of the walk: 3 ½ miles. Map: OS Outdoor Leisure 24 White Peak Area (inn GR 348516).

This route offers you canalside walking. The Cromford Canal is full of wildlife – moorhens are seen regularly and you may even be lucky enough to spot a kingfisher. Look out as well for the odd pike lying just below the surface of the water, waiting for its prey to pass unsuspectingly by. A fairly steady climb brings you out on the hillside above the Derwent valley, giving you some impressive views before you descend back to the valley bottom.

The Walk

From the car park walk to the A6, with the hotel on your right. Cross the road and turn left towards Matlock. Just over 250 yards from the hotel is a house called Alandale on your right. Immediately past this, turn right along Chase Road – a signpost points towards Bullbridge and Fritchley. Within 50 yards pass under the railway bridge. Stay on the tarmac lane to pass the house known as South Bridge on your right. You then reach another bridge. Do not cross it. You need to get onto the canal towpath, so take the step-over stile beside the gate to the left of the bridge. Turn left along the canal.

Walk on the towpath, with the canal to your right, for 250 yards. Pass under a bridge. Turn left here to cross over the bridge you have just walked

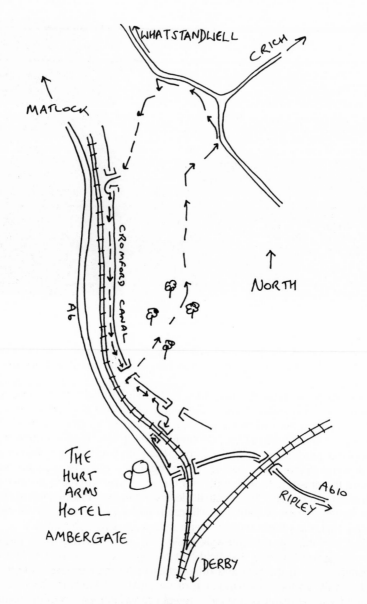

WHATSTANDWELL

CRICH

MATLOCK

A6

CROMFORD CANAL

NORTH

THE
HURT
ARMS
HOTEL

AMBERGATE

A610

RIPLEY

DERBY

under. Once you have crossed this, turn left almost immediately to enter a field by a farm gate. Just to the right of this gate is a water trough set below ground level with steps leading down to it. When you are in the field turn right and walk up it. In the top corner is a squeezer stile. Pass through this

Cromford canal.

into the wood. Walk straight ahead on the distinct, sunken path in front. If there are fallen trees across it you may have to make small detours around them.

You reach a level, grassy 'ride' running from left to right across your path. Ignore this and continue forward along the obvious path into the trees. Subsequently, pass through a gateway to come to an open, grassy, area. Staying on the left side of this, continue forward. This leads you into more woodland, predominantly silver birches. The path levels out and then begins to descend slightly. After passing to the right of a gatepost the path forks. Ignore the grassy path descending to the left – take the more distinct one rising in front of you. This eventually levels out to pass through ferns. Along this straight length of path you will catch glimpses, to your left, of Alder-wasley Hall, the white building over a mile away across the valley.

The view improves as you walk beside two fields on your right. (Ignore the stile going into the first field.) At the end of the second field cross through a gap in the wall and turn right to take the step-over stile in the fence. Walk up the right-hand side of the next two fields to the road. To your left can be seen Crich Stand, a tower erected in memory of the soldiers of the Sherwood Foresters and Worcestershire Regiment who have died in battle. Turn left at Chadwick Nick Lane. There is no jail here, just a gap – a 'nick' – in the ridge of rocks 200 yards uphill to the right.

Walk left on the lane for just over 100 yards, ignoring a squeezer stile immediately beyond the largish green gas board 'box'. The stile you are looking for is just a few yards before a small metal gate on the left. Pass through the stile and walk half-right, through the narrow wood, to the stile ahead. Pass through this into the field. Cross the corner of the field to the stile 25 yards away. Enter a second field and walk half-left across it. Aim to the left of the tree jutting out into the field. Then follow the edge of the wood round to the right to reach the road. Turn left to walk down this for 400 yards. There is no pavement, so take care. The footpath you need from the road is on the left-hand side of the right-hand bend. Take care here – it may be best to get on the left side of the road before the bend. Pass through the squeezer stile on the left in the wall, just beyond the house known as Chase Cliffe. Look for the rather fine deer on the top of the building.

The signpost points into the trees. Follow the well-used path and walk alongside a wall to descend to a track. Turn left for about 600 yards. Ignoring all tracks and paths to left and right, stay on the main track until you reach the canal again. Cross this by the bridge, then turn left immediately by the step-over stile. Walk down to the canal. With it on your left, walk for a mile to a stone bridge and go under this. Some 250 yards later you reach another bridge. This is where you originally got onto the towpath. Turn right here off the towpath and onto the tarmac lane, then turn right down the lane to get back to the A6. Once you reach the main road turn left back to the Hurt Arms Hotel.

16 Duffield
The White Hart

The village of Duffield (Duvelle in Domesday, meaning the place where there are doves) is a few miles north of Derby on the A6. The White Hart is a relatively 'young' pub, being opened on Good Friday, 1939. The original landlord was George Thornewell, an ex-Derby County footballer.

This comfortable inn, with its oak-panelled rooms, provides good, home-cooked, traditional food and is very popular with local people. It provides good value for money. Besides sandwiches, such as salmon, prawn and steak, the menu includes steak and kidney pie, fisherman's pie, scampi, grilled salmon steak with herb butter, vegetarian lasagne, chicken à la king and gammon, egg and pineapple. For the 'Young at Hart', there are such delights as sausage, beefburger, scampi or chicken nuggets, all with chips. There is also a family room. Pedigree and Bass real ale is sold, and Strongbow cider. There is an attractive garden for those summer days when the sun shines and a pint of beer is what you crave.

The White Hart is open from Monday to Saturday from 11.30 am until 2.30 pm and from 6 pm to 11 pm. It opens on Sundays during the usual hours. Food is served from noon until 2 pm daily and from 6 pm until 9 pm on Wednesday to Saturday. There is no food on Sunday, Monday and Tuesday evenings.

Telephone: 01332 841141.

How to get there: The White Hart is beside the A6, in the middle of Duffield, about 4 miles north of Derby.

Parking: Space should be available in the pub car parks – one is in front of the pub and the other behind. Please ask before leaving your car there while you walk. There is parking available in some streets nearby.

Length of the walk: 4 miles. OS Pathfinder 811 Belper (inn GR 345433).

This is a town and country walk through the green and pleasant land that is Middle England. The start and finish of the route is through Duffield village and the meat in the sandwich is the chance to find a little peace and quiet in the Ecclesbourne valley. The Ecclesbourne is not so much over-looked by many walkers as completely unknown to them.

The Walk

Standing in front of the White Hart, turn left along the A6. Stay on the left side of the road, past the shops and post office. Some 100 yards from the pub look out for Chapel Street, across the road on the right. Turn left here along the road, with the river Ecclesbourne on the right. After 100 yards, follow the road round to the right and cross the river. Then follow the road left, passing Bridge Cottage and various red-brick houses on your left. Facing you on the house at the end of the street is a sign saying 'Crown Street'. Bear left in front of this – the river is over the wall on your left now. Within 100 yards, on your left, is Kingfisher Cottage. Turn left immediately beyond this, through the stone stoops. Follow the path alongside the river on your left.

Walk along the path to a narrowish tarmac drive, then pass a children's playground on your right. The drive bears left to a bridge. Cross this and another bridge 60 yards later. After the second bridge keep straight on, passing a school on your right. About 150 yards beyond the school entrance turn right at some shops along Meadow Vale and, 200 yards later, left into Ferrers Crescent. Follow this slightly uphill and then round to the right. Turn left on the path between nos 35 and 37. This leads to Wirksworth Road after 100 yards. Cross to the signpost marked 'Woodfall Lane' and 'Cum-berhill'. This is just left of Broom Park Lodge.

Follow the path into a field. Walk up the right side of this and a second field. At the top of the second field cross the stile (or pass through the gate beside it). Walk directly towards the poles on the skyline. You reach a track running from left to right before the overhead lines. Turn right along this towards Champion Farm. The farmhouse is interesting because of its unusual symmetrical shape. This is the highest point of the walk and affords wide views of the Ecclesbourne valley and Duffield. To the right of the farm there is a large field. Some locals believe that grapes to make champagne

74

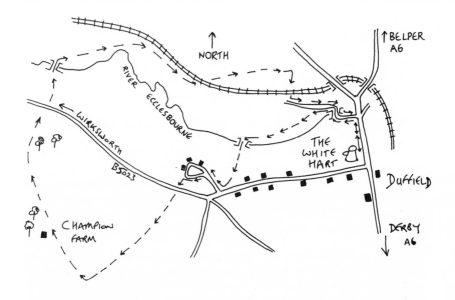

were grown here centuries ago, hence Champion Farm. The likely explanation, however, is simpler – 'Champion' derives from the old French 'Champaigne' meaning 'open country'.

Stay on the gravel track alongside a wood on your left. At the end of the wood pass through a gate. This area is full of wildlife. If this route is walked around September/October look out for the pheasants. I once saw over 30 birds within 40 yards of the track.

Continue to descend along the track (which gets grassier), with a wood on your right. Just before a second gate look out for the smallish wood ahead, to the left. You may be able to pick out the raised earthworks of an ancient moat beneath the trees. Centuries ago a fairly substantial building stood here – now there is nothing but a grassy bank. Pass through the second gate and follow the track as it bears right. Keep straight ahead towards the red-brick house, 350 yards away down the track.

At the house pass through two gates to reach Wirksworth road again. Cross half-right to the signpost opposite. Climb the stile and walk on the right side of the field away from the road. In the second field walk slightly left towards a bridge, 150 yards away across the field. Cross this and pass through the gateway in front. Ignore the stile and gate to your left. Once through the gateway, walk half-right across the field. The stile you want is 70 yards to the right of the top corner of the field. Cross the stile beside the river and walk through the next field under the electricity cables. At the end of the field go through a gap in the hedge. Walk forward alongside the hedge down the left side of the third field. Pass through a gap at the end,

then through a squeezer 50 yards later. This brings you into a long, narrow field with factory buildings at the far end.

Some 100 yards into the field climb a substantial stile on the left. Cross the railway line. The sign says 'STOP LOOK AND LISTEN'. The line does not appear to have been used for some time, but heed these words – just in case. Today could be the day British Rail runs a Special up the line to Wirksworth! Cross the line and the step-over beyond. Turn half-right in the field to the gap in the hedge. In the second field walk directly away from the stile. Ignore a path heading half-left from the stile and another path half-left partway across the field. At the far side of the field, cross the footbridge and stile, then walk half-left to the far left corner near the cemetery.

Climb the solid wooden step-over and keep on the path for 100 yards. Under a conker tree the path bears half-left between fences and hedges to a driveway 70 yards later. Cross this and walk downhill alongside a wall on your left. About 200 yards later re-cross the railway line to a road. Turn left for 300 yards, passing Snake Lane on the right. You will see at the far end that the road you are on is Holloway Road. It brings you back to Kingfisher Cottage. Look out for Yew Tree Cottage, opposite, with the interesting old insurance company fire mark on the front of the house.

Continue along the road, bearing right just beyond the post box on your right. You are now returning to the White Hart on your outward route. So, walk alongside the red-brick houses on your right. With Brook Cottage ahead at the end of the street, turn right over the Ecclesbourne. Bear left back to the A6 and then right to return to the pub.

17 Horsley
The Coach and Horses

Horsley village used to be one of the most important settlements in the area – with Horsley Castle nearby. The castle was eventually demolished, with the stone apparently being taken to build Kedleston Hall, 5 miles away to the south-west. In this attractive village are three stone fountains bestowed by a local minister in the mid 19th century. They were named after each of his three daughters. Two of the names are plainly discernible – Blanche and Sophia – the other, on the small green near the pub, less so. The Coach and Horses, the sole remaining hostelry in the village, was built by William Shaw in 1717 and was originally the local court house. It is said that many condemned men were actually hanged in what is now the lounge. The only spirits around, however, are those on sale behind the bar.

Like so many pubs nowadays, the Coach and Horses offers good value for money. The food available is home cooked and includes favourites such as steak and kidney pie, chilli con carne, lasagne, chicken Kiev, seafood platter, breaded plaice, scampi and cod plus sizzling pepper steaks. There are usually a couple of vegetarian meals on offer. The children's menu comprises fish fingers, chicken nuggets, sausages or a child's portion of the roast of the day. Some walkers are perhaps more interested in the real ale than the food, so, for them, Marston's Pedigree and Bitter are available as well as

Bateman Champion Dark Mild. In addition, a guest traditional ale is usually on offer. Cider drinkers can try the Bulmers Original which is on draught. The pub has a children's play area and a beer garden.

The pub opens from 11.30 am until 3 pm and from 6 pm until 11 pm Monday to Saturday. The usual times apply on Sunday. Food is available from 11.30 am (noon on Sunday) until 2.30 pm and from 6 pm until 8 pm every evening except Sunday.

Telephone: 01332 880581.

How to get there: Horsley can be reached from the A609 Belper to Ilkeston road. In the village of Kilburn look out for the Horsley (not Horsley Woodhouse) signs. Horsley is about 1 mile south of Kilburn. The Coach and Horses is at one end of Church Street and the church is at the other.

Parking: You can park in the pub car park while you walk, provided you have a word with the landlord first. Alternatively, there is parking available on the road in the village.

Length of the walk: 3 miles. Map: OS Pathfinder 811 Belper (inn GR 381445).

This short walk is close to the A38 but demonstrates how lucky the folk of Derbyshire are in their county. The walk passes through an attractive area, well known to locals but largely unexplored.

The Walk

Facing away from the Coach and Horses, walk right along the main street in the village. Notice the old stone fountains as you go. Also look out for the 19th century pillarbox at the end of French Lane. This appears to be unique. After about 500 yards you come to the church. Turn left at the signpost, to 'Coxbench', at the side of the gate into the churchyard. At the end of the churchyard bear slightly left towards the electricity pylon across the field. Do not walk towards the other pylon down the wallside in front of you. Pass through the broken hawthorn hedge. Before you reach the pylon walk diagonally across the field to the top corner. Once through the squeezer stile bear half-right towards the red-brick house. The path takes you to the right of this, through a hedge and a kissing-gate. Keep forward to the gate to the left of the corrugated-sheet barn. Once through the gate keep forward to the far left-hand corner of the field. Climb the stile and proceed down the steps at the side of the cottage to the lane. Turn right along here. Just beyond Greengates Cottage (at the side of Holly Cottage) keep straight ahead to descend the path alongside the hedge.

Once out on Horsley Lane turn right. About 50 yards later you reach St Anthony's Well, Coxbench. This was erected in 1611 in a cottage garden but

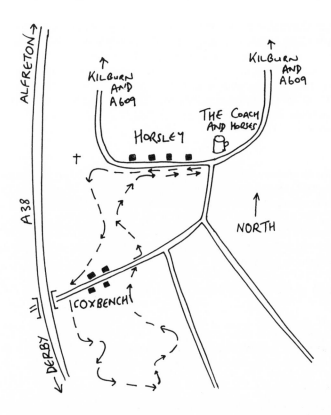

moved to its present site in 1979. It was regularly used by monks and the water was alleged to have healing qualities. Unfortunately, nothing runs from it now.

Above you is the A38. Cross directly over the road you are on to walk up the lane opposite. This is signposted 'Sandy Lane', although it is not very clear to read. Stay on the lane (ignoring a track to the left). It rises round to the left. At the side of a driveway leading through the trees, climb the step-over stile onto the path running parallel to the drive for a short distance. This path goes between fences. At the end of the fencing walk along the top side of a field. Just before the end of the hedge cross the step-over stile on your right. (Do not continue through the field under the electricity lines.) The path ascends slowly alongside a fence to your right. Where the wood leads uphill to your left, ignore this path but stay on the one along the hedgeside. This then bears left uphill with the fence. During sunny days in summertime this wood is full of wood ants – watch where you sit if you want a breather. Slowly the noise of the A38 recedes as you walk away from it.

'Blanche' – one of the three stone fountains in Horsley.

The ruins of Horsley Castle are in the vicinity, although none are visible from the path. Keep a disused quarry on your left. Where the path forks, keep along the more distinct path on the right. This runs along the top of a bank falling away to the right. Go between two wooden gateposts and a stone post before joining a path running from left to right in front of you. A lovely view of Horsley and beyond opens out. Turn right. About 175 yards later the path bears round to the right. Pass through the gate on your left just before the bend. Walk half-left towards the gate to the left of the pylon. As you walk towards it you may be able to see Crich Stand just to the right of the pylon. This is just under 8 miles away.

Once through the squeezer stile beside the gate walk down the left side of the field towards another squeezer stile. Do not pass through this, though – turn right to walk towards the church on the hillside opposite. The path is fairly clear, although originally it would appear to have been a sunken lane on your left. Cross Park Brook by an old stone slab bridge, then head towards the stile in front. Turn right once you are on the road. Walk 30 yards or so beyond Keeper's Cottage on the left. Look out for the signpost pointing towards a stile. Climb the steps to it and squeeeeeze through – it's narrow. Walk up the right side of the field, then cross a second field. In a third field pass under the electricity cables and continue towards the church. You will arrive back at the pylon you walked towards (from the churchyard) earlier.

After passing through the gap keep on the right of the field to pass an orchard and farm buildings. Ignore a stile on your right which leads into the farmyard near the haybarn. Beyond this stile, about 30 yards before the gate at the end of the field, look for a narrow squeezer stile on your right. Pass through and walk to the far left corner of the small field. Once in the corner turn left. Walk between gardens and return to the main street. From here, turn right to walk back to the Coach and Horses.

18 Ednaston
The Yew Tree Inn

Motorists hurtling by on the A52 just a few hundred yards away probably have little idea about the village and its inn. With its red-brick houses and the fascinating church to the east, Ednaston is well worth exploring.

The Yew Tree Inn, complete with its own yew tree, started life as an alehouse in the 18th century. Two centuries later it is still in the same business, catering for the needs of anyone wanting food or drink. There are plenty of dishes to choose from. The normal menu includes lasagne, battered haddock, steak and kidney pie and chilli con carne, but there are also items like smoked salmon and prawn platter, chicken Kiev and broccoli and cream cheese bake. Then the specials (shown on the blackboard) may be such things as lamb curry or beef with black pepper sauce. There is also a roast for Sunday lunch. Children can have smaller portions of anything. When meals are not being served rolls and beverages are available. The inn has barbecues during the summer on Saturday and Sunday evenings – if the weather is fit. As regards beer, there is always a guest beer on offer, plus Bass and Pedigree. Caffery's Ale is also sold, as well as Guinness and Murphy's stout. Cider drinkers are catered for with Strongbow and Woodpecker. If you still have some energy after your walk and meal you might like to try a game of darts, dominoes or pool.

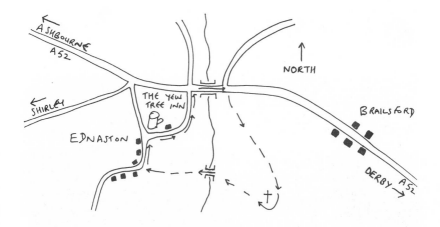

On Monday to Saturday the inn is open for 12 hours – from 11 am to 11 pm, with the usual hours on a Sunday. Each day meals are served from noon to 2.30 pm and 6 pm to 9 pm – there are no meals available on Sunday evening.

Telephone: 01335 360433.

How to get there: Ednaston is signed from the A52 Derby to Ashbourne road, 1 mile to the west of Brailsford. The inn is easy to find in the village.

Parking: You can park at the inn while you walk, but let the landlady know first please.

Length of the walk: 1½ miles. Map: OS Pathfinder 811 Belper (inn GR 239415).

This is the shortest walk in the book. It is well worth while, though, because it leads to Brailsford church. This stands on the hillside above the village and is a fascinating place to visit – one of those places that people are likely to revisit once they have discovered it.

The Walk

From the Yew Tree car park turn left. After 100 yards follow the lane round to the left and stay on it for another 350 yards or so. This brings you to the busy A52. Cross this carefully to the pavement on the opposite side of the road and turn right. Walk along the pavement for 200 yards, crossing Brailsford Brook by the roadbridge. Just beyond the bridge cross the road to the public bridleway sign opposite. Follow the tarmac bridleway for 150 yards until it forks. The left fork leads up to Church Farm. Keep straight

Brailsford church.

ahead along the track, with the garden hedge on your left. Pass through the
wooden farm gate in front of you at the end of the hedge. There is a distinct
bridleway which eventually leads through gorse bushes before opening out
on the left-hand side.

Stay on the bridleway as it rises alongside the hedgerow. After a few
hundred yards it brings you to Brailsford church. Continue through the
parking area, with the church to your right, to the far end of the churchyard.
Just beyond the churchyard there is an 18th century red-brick stable. A stone
above the entrance shows 'This stable was built at ye expense and for the
use of the parish in 1754'. What a delightful building, but what a pity there is
an electricity pole right at the side of it. From the gate between the stable
and the stone mounting block, walk forward into the churchyard towards
the church porch. Just before you reach the porch there is a medieval cross
base. Underneath this, in July 1919, the shaft of an ancient cross was found.
This has now been mounted on a stone beside the base. The figure of a
man with a sword can be clearly seen. Sadly, the church is usually locked.
Above the entrance the date '1629' is engraved, as well as the initials 'WM'
and 'EB'. There is also an old sundial on the porch.

Initially, one may be tempted to think that this church served a com-
munity in the fields surrounding the churchyard and that the village dis-
appeared, like so many others in medieval times, due to the plague or some
other disaster. This is, in fact, not the case. The church actually served the

village of Brailsford on one side and Ednaston on the other. In ancient documents both villages are described as having half a church each, that is, one between them. The bridleway and paths that converge on the church are evidence of this being a focal point for the villages in days gone by. Some of these paths are regularly ploughed up and not reinstated but eventually it is to be hoped that these old rights of way will be treated with the respect they merit.

From the porch continue along the path, with the church on your right. You reach a metal gate which was erected in memory of Constance Brindley 'who liked this quiet place'. Follow the path to the bottom of the field, then bear right to cross Brailsford Brook again. This time the bridge is far smaller than the one you used to cross the brook before. This is another lovely, serene place. Follow the distinct path away from the brook to a stile and climb into the field. Walk up the field to the top left-hand corner. There is a stile just to the left of the red-brick building. Walk along the left side of the building to another squeezer stile, 40 yards away.

Turn right along the lane, passing Ednaston House on your right. Then pass Swan Cottage on the left, just before the Yew Tree.

19 Repton
The Bulls Head

Repton is a fascinating place. The name originated from a tribe of people known as the Hreope. The village was presumably the 'Hill of the Hreope' ('dun' means hill), so 'Hreope-dun' was corrupted over the years to Repton. The High Street and church are full of interest.

The Bulls Head is a large, imposing building with a friendly welcome and an appealing atmosphere. The flagstones in the pub are 16th century – the restaurant area was originally stables. The auction posters, framed Victorian cartoons and old invoices all add interest to the pub. It is the sort of place where you can happily pass the time eating, drinking and savouring the character of the place. While you're doing this the children can play outside in the play area. Foodwise, 'Sammy Squirrel's Children's Specials' are on offer for the under 11s. There are also suitable sweets, including ice-cream. Mum and Dad are certainly not overlooked – there is a wide choice available. Besides the specials (like home-made brewer's pie, country vegetable and cheese bake, and broccoli and cream cheese bake), there are starters such as Tex Mex tortillas with chilli and melted cheese, or home-made soup with bread. The main course features items like beef, mushroom and ale pie, scampi, rump steak, chicken kebab and chicken Kiev. Snacks can also be purchased, for example, Bulls Head toasties and ploughman's lunches.

The drinks that are available are Draught Burton Ale, Marstons Pedigree and Bass bitter. In addition Gaymer's Olde English Cider is on offer. Opening times – food is served every day from noon until 2 pm. Then every evening (except Sunday) food is available from 6 pm until 9.30 pm. The pub is open for drinks from noon until 2.30 pm and 6 pm until 11 pm every day of the week except for Sunday when the normal times apply. The Bulls Head also offers overnight accommodation.

Telephone: 01283 703297.

How to get there: Repton lies on the B5008, 7 miles south-west of the centre of Derby. From the A38 Burton upon Trent to Derby road follow the signs for Willington and then Repton. The Bulls Head is in High Street.

Parking: During your walk, leave your car in the pub car park (after you've asked) or park in the village.

Length of the walk: 4 ¾ miles. Map: OS Pathfinder 852 Burton upon Trent (inn GR 306266).

A flat walk – nothing strenuous. The route takes you from Repton to the charming village of Newton Solney and back. The path that returns to Repton above the Trent is usually bristling with wildlife in summer.

The Walk

With your back to the Bulls Head, turn left along High Street. Turn left at the road known as The Pastures and walk along it for 100 yards. Where it bears right and then left follow it round to the right and keep going – ignore the rest of the road to the left. Walk along the narrower tarmac cul-de-sac for 60 yards beside a 6 ft high wooden fence. Beyond the house numbered '20' and with Silverdene on your right, turn left and walk along the path behind the houses, for 300 yards. Cross a stile, then pass through a kissing-gate to reach a road. Bear left for 100 yards, to where it ends in a cul-de-sac.

Pass through the stone stoops, ignoring the track to the left. Walk alongside the fence. Cross the stile at the end of the field. Keep on the right side of the second field, then cross another stile to walk between hedges. The path becomes a track. Turn right towards a brick farmhouse 300 yards ahead. About 120 yards later, turn left along another track with the farm-house to your right. Stay on this track for ½ mile.

When the track bears left to a house, head forward down the right-hand side of the field ahead. Some 30 yards later, cross a stile. Continue forward over another stile, then walk towards the left-hand side of the trees ahead. Go round these to where three tracks join. Cross the stile and walk up the right-hand side of the field ahead for ½ mile to the road. This large field was originally three fields. Before the lane turn round and admire the view.

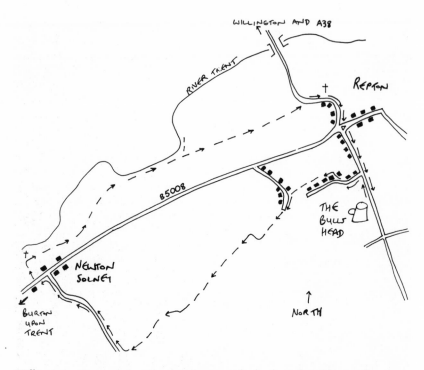

Willington power station is prominent, with the long low Toyota factory to the left.

Turn right along the lane towards Newton Solney, ½ mile away. Follow the lane round a right-hand bend, passing Green Bank Cottage on your left. Take care here – walk on the outside of the bend. Continue into this attractive village. Turn left at the grass triangle towards the Brickmakers' Arms and the interesting pub sign. About 100 yards beyond the pub, turn right down Church Lane past Beehive Cottage. Enter the churchyard by the kissing-gate, then turn right to walk between the slate gravestones towards another kissing-gate. Continue along the tarmac path, out of the churchyard. Descend the steps to a road. Continue into Blacksmith Lane. After 120 yards bear left towards Newton Close, then turn right into Cricket Close. Walk to the far end climbing the stile into the field to the right of no 17. Willington is 2 miles away.

Walk slightly right of the tree ahead. Beyond is a stile into the next field. From this stile walk half-left towards the gate in the left-hand hedge – between you and the power station. Bear slightly left in the third field, aiming to the right of what resembles a grey footbridge about ½ mile away. (It is in fact an arched pipe.) This brings you to a stile in the hedge. Cross towards another hedge and trees ahead.

Newton Solney church.

Go over a footbridge and stay on the left side of the field, with the stream to your left. The path runs along the top of an embankment falling away to the left. The river Trent can be seen now, although better views are visible shortly. Cross a stile beside a gate and 10 yards beyond, pass through another gate. A track descends slightly left here. Ignore this and keep forward along the flattish ground ahead. Continue without losing height, with the hedge on your right. Ignore a concrete stile on your right a little later. Views of the Trent improve. Stay on the fairly clear path, with a hedge or fence on your right. I have seen seagulls, geese, cormorant, butterflies and beautiful damselflies in this area.

Eventually, at the end of the barbed wire fence the path crosses a stile. Keep left beside the trees. Ahead is the 200 ft spire of Repton church ⅔ mile away. Keep forward at the end of the trees to the stile ahead, ignoring the stile on your left down to the river. In the next field keep forward, with the fence on your right. Pass a hollow on your left and bear left beyond it. Almost immediately, turn right alongside the hedge on your right. When you come to a more open, bumpy, field, stay on the right of this. Away to your right is a red-brick farmhouse. Pass through a narrow stile and continue forward, with a fence on your left, towards the church. What a contrast between the church spire ahead and the power station! Pass through a gateway at the end of the hedge. Walk down the field towards the pebble-dashed house (dated 1905) at the end. About 20 yards before the end turn left through the stile in the hedge. Walk down the steps, then turn right along the lane. Branch slightly left before Homelea. The path leads past tennis courts. At the end of the path cross the road. Turn right and follow the road round to the left to reach the churchyard on your left, with thatched cottages opposite. The church is well worth exploring, especially if the crypt is open.

Bear right from the church towards the town cross. Here in the 19th century a man offered his wife for sale for one shilling. Keep just left of the cross to walk along High Street, directly away from the church. Pass Repton post office and other interesting buildings to return to the pub.

20 **Hartshorne**
The Bulls Head

Hartshorne lies in the pleasant countryside between Derby and Burton upon Trent. It is quite a small, relatively modern village, with one or two older properties including the Bulls Head.

The Bulls Head is an attractive red-brick building and a friendly, cosy pub. Judging by the number of people there at all times in the week, it is a favourite eating place.

There is a wide choice of food. The meals are fairly priced and include scampi, trout and chicken chasseur, sirloin chasseur and Stilton gammon. The vegetarian dishes are, for example, vegetable lasagne, vegetable curry and mushrooms in garlic and tomato sauce. There are snacks, too, such as 4 oz beefburger, cheeseburger and bacon or sausage cob. Salads are also available. Children can order half of most things on the menu. The pub sells Burtonwood Top Hat and Bitter, plus James Forshaw's Bitter, for devotees of real ale, and Strongbow cider. The Bulls Head offers overnight accommodation.

The pub opens from 11 am until 3 pm and from 6.30 pm until 11 pm on Monday to Saturday, with the usual hours on a Sunday. Meals are available from noon until 2 pm and from 7 pm until 9.30 pm daily.

Telephone: 01283 215299.

How to get there: Hartshorne lies between Ticknall and Woodville, on the A514 south of Derby. The Bulls Head is at the south end of the village, near the church.

Parking: Feel free to park in front of the pub or, preferably, in the larger car park nearby. Alternatively park lower down in the village, on the road.

Length of the walk: 3 ½ miles (a short cut is available, for a shorter walk). Map: OS Pathfinder 852 Burton upon Trent (inn GR 327207).

This is a walk in an area probably unknown to 99% of the walkers in Derbyshire and it is a pity that places like Hartshorne aren't visited more often. However, South Derbyshire District Council are opening up obstructed paths and waymarking them. They also produce footpath leaflets highlighting circuits around various villages. Part of this route has been opened up by the Council. It takes you through rolling countryside and woodland, as well as the village.

The Walk

From the car park in front of the Bulls Head, turn right to ascend the road alongside the pub and pass the larger car park on the left. Some 100 yards later turn left along the track signposted 'Smisby 2 miles'. Follow the track as it bends right, 200 yards later arriving at a large field. Walk 400 yards across this – aim just left of the buildings on the horizon ahead – keep in single file if there is a crop. As you proceed look out for the 8 ft high signpost ahead. From this, bear slightly right across the field towards the buildings on the hilltop ahead. Walk just left of the willow tree at the bottom of the hedge running downhill from the right. An obvious path leads into the wood.

This brings you to a delightful spot – a secluded pond. In summertime the area is alive with insects and birds. Cross a stile and walk across the field towards another wood, 350 yards away. Keep the tree in the middle of the field on your left, then walk between a second tree and the banking on your right. Climb the stile into the wood. Some 5 yards later, turn left along the distinct path. This runs through the wood for 150 yards. Look out, 40 yards before the end of the wood, for a drop on your left into the stream. This is 8 ft below the path and can be missed amongst the undergrowth. The path through the wood is far from the madding crowd, which is, of course, one of the reasons for getting out into the country in the first place.

At the edge of the wood cross the stile, then turn right to walk alongside the wood. Cross the stile at the end of the field. Turn left to walk away from the wood to a stile 175 yards later. Turn left along the track. You have now walked round three sides of an oblong. Keep straight on in the next field towards a gate. After crossing the stile beside it, continue forward, beside

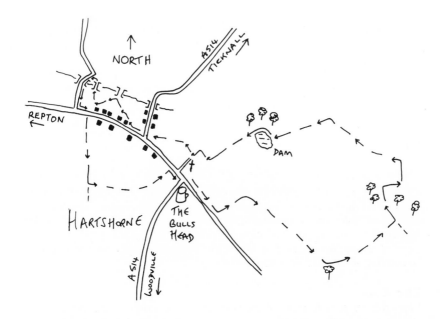

the broken line of trees. For the next 450 yards walk along the bottom of a
bank to your right. Pass through another line of trees running downhill to
your left. Hartshorne church is visible ½ mile ahead. Stay on the top side of
the next field until you reach the end. Bear slightly right alongside a fence
on the left and, 100 yards later, cross a stile on your left. Walk down the
right-hand side of the field in the direction of the church towards the wood.
Continue into the bottom corner, ignoring the track running from left to
right just before this. The path turns right to descend into trees, with
Limehouse Dam on your left. Turn left beside the dam. Follow the path out
into a field. Ascend alongside a hedge on your right for 300 yards and cross
a farm track and a stile.

Continue forward, with the hedge still on your right. Some 15 yards
before the corner of the field the hedge bends right slightly. Round this
bend, out of sight, is a stile (just a few yards beyond a 15 yard gap in the
hedge). Cross the stile and walk down the left side of the field. Climb the
fence stile beside a metal gate and walk past a bungalow on your right, to an
access road. Turn left along this for 50 yards beside the field below to the
right.

For a short cut, if you continue along the track you pass the church to
arrive at the main road. Turn left to return to the Bulls Head.

For the main walk, turn sharp right over the stile on your right at the end
of the field. Walk down the left side of the field. Cross the stile beside the

Nosey cows!

gate at the bottom and head half-left to the gates 200 yards away. After passing through two gates, you reach the road. Watch out for traffic here. Take the middle of the three roads available at this point – the Repton road – and walk down it for 100 yards.

Turn right at the signpost for Spring Hill, pass between the houses and go through a kissing-gate. With your back to the brick wall beside the kissing-gate, walk half-left across the field, keeping just right of the fenced square for training horses. Pass through the gate at the side of this. The next stile is 100 yards ahead, on the left-hand side of the field. The path does not actually go in a straight line to this stile, however, but descends to the bridge on your right before rising and continuing through the field you are in, to the stile. (Remember – do not cross the bridge.)

Cross the stile and follow the path, then turn right to cross the stream. This path runs beside an attractive garden to the road. Turn left to a grass triangle 200 yards later. Turn left along the road for 50 yards and cross over to the signpost, 'Woodville 1 ½ miles'. Follow this path, climb a stile and continue down the right side of the field for 200 yards. Cross another stile and proceed for another 200 yards keeping 40 yards to the right of the field boundary on your left. Approximately 30 yards beyond the power line climb the stile on the left. This is 15 yards or so before the first of two metal gates on the left-hand side of the field. After crossing it, walk up the right side of the field.

At the top, cross the stile and bear slightly left. Keep 30 yards left of the enclosure in the middle of the field. Walk to the kissing-gate to the left of a farm gate. Follow the gravel path to the left to a small playing field. Walk to the far right corner, passing a playground. Beyond this turn right up the road to the Bulls Head. Cross to the left side of the road before you reach the pub, to avoid crossing the road on the dangerous bend directly in front of it.